P9-DTQ-606

THE POPULAR
POTATO
BEST RECIPES

VALWYN McMONIGAL

TORMONT

CONTENTS

Photography by Ashley Barber
Styling by Michelle Gorry

This edition is published with the permission of HarperCollins Publishers Pty Limited.

Published in 1993 by
Tormont Publications Inc.
338 Saint Antoine St. East
Montreal, Canada H2Y 1A3
Tel. (514) 954-1441
Fax (514) 954-1443
ISBN 2-89429-392-5
Printed in Canada

Text Copyright © Valwyn McMonigal, 1989
Apart from any fair dealing for the purposes of private study, research, criticism or review, as permitted under the Copyright Act, no part may be reproduced by any process without written permission.

ACKNOWLEDGEMENTS
The publisher would like to thank the following for their help during the photography of this book:
Accoutrement; Appley Hoare Antiques; Corso de Fiori; Casa Shopping Exclusive Kitchen and Giftware; Chelsea House Antiques; Country Collection; Country Form Furniture; Dansab Pty Ltd; John Normyle; Laura Ashley (Aust) Pty Ltd, Lesolivades; Lifestyle Imports Pty Ltd; Made Where; Mikasa Tableware; Parterre Garden; Royal Doulton Australia Pty Ltd; Saywell Imports; Sydney Antique Centre; The Bay Tree; The Country Trader.

All About Potatoes

Historical Background

The potato has a remarkable history. It has been baked, boiled, steamed and mashed, used as a diet food and loved by diabetics. It has also been blamed for causing leprosy and mass emigration, and its flowers have decorated royal coat lapels and crockery.

Colloquially known as the 'spud' — the name of the tool once used to weed the potato patch — the potato is one of the most popular staple foods in the world. Eaten since ancient times, it still graces most plates at least once a day in many countries.

The known history of potato cultivation in South America began 1800 years ago. Its introduction to Europe is more recent. In 1500 AD, the Spanish reached the Andes in Peru and christened the potato the 'batata,' the West Indian name for the botanically quite distinct sweet potato.

Reports as to how potatoes reached Europe vary. Some claim they came in a Spanish Armada ship which foundered in Irish waters in the mid-16th century. Sir John Hawkins is reputed to have introduced the potato to England in 1563, but cultivation did not begin until Sir Francis Drake brought back another load of potatoes in 1586.

Popular history credits Sir Walter Raleigh with the introduction of potato cultivation in Ireland and the humble 'spud' reached the royal table in England in 1619. By the 18th century, the potato had traveled to North America, and was being grown in England, Scotland, Ireland, France and Germany.

The potato's reputation did suffer some blows on the way. In France, until the late 1700s, it was widely believed that the potato caused leprosy and fever. In 1773, the French scientist Parmentier wrote a thesis extolling the virtues of the potato. Following the success of a royal grant to encourage potato cultivation, King Louis XVI is reported to have worn a potato flower in his buttonhole.

Scorn turned to praise and the potato flower became highly fashionable, decorating everything from clothing to crockery. By the early 19th century, the potato had become a staple food in France.

The Irish also embraced the potato, so enthusiastically that their economy soon became dependent on it. The Irish potato crop of 1845–1847 failed disastrously due to blight, causing starvation and mass emigration to the United States and Australia. Settlers brought their love of potatoes with them and the development of new varieties and anti-fungal chemicals guaranteed continued cultivation.

The popularity of the potato has grown steadily over the years. Potatoes are used to make bread in many countries, eaten as a vegetable every day around the world, and, recently, restaurants specializing in every imaginable kind of potato dish have become spectacularly fashionable in New York and London.

Nutritional Value
One of the main reasons for the popularity of the potato is its excellent nutritional value. With a high water content, it makes a filling bulk food. It has a good ratio of proteins to calories and the quality of those proteins is high. There is also a high level of vitamins and minerals.

The average baked potato provides the recommended daily intake of riboflavin (vitamin B_2), three to four times the necessary amount of thiamin (vitamin B_1) and niacin (vitamin B_3), one and a half times the quantity of iron, and ten times the amount of vitamin C.

It has almost no fat or salt and offers more potassium than a banana. It is one of the easiest types of starch to assimilate and contains two and half times fewer carbohydrates than a similar quantity of bread, which makes the potato popular with diabetics.

It is also becoming a popular diet food. Because of traditional toppings such as sour cream and butter, the potato has developed a reputation as a no-no for weight watchers. In reality, a fair-sized baked potato (7 oz or 200 g) contains about the same number of calories (kilojoules) as an average apple or a glass of orange juice (about 72 Cal or 300 kj).

POTATO TO FUEL THE CAR
In 1917, Henry Ford suggested that a potato from Europe with a high-yielding alcohol content should be grown and used in place of gasoline!

Types, Preparation and Cooking Techniques

Types

The way potatoes are cooked is only limited by the cook's imagination. However, not all ways of cooking suit all types of potatoes; so the type of potatoes you buy should depend on how you plan to cook them.

Extensive research is being undertaken around the world and there are now literally hundreds of varieties: white, yellow, red, purple and lilac. What is available in your grocery store depends on where you live, however, as different varieties are grown in different countries.

Many people know the potatoes they buy only by the classifications of 'red,' 'old' and 'new.' Red are usually a red-skinned type, such as Pontiac, but old and new refer to the stages of growth: new potatoes are the latest season's crop; old potatoes are from the previous year.

The following is a short list of some of the more popular varieties available:

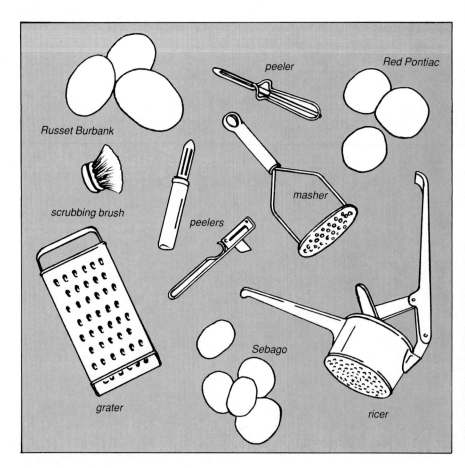

Russet Burbank · peeler · Red Pontiac · scrubbing brush · peelers · masher · grater · Sebago · ricer

6

WHAT POTATO IS THAT?

TYPE	DESCRIPTION	PERFORMANCE IN			
		boiling	baking	frying	salads
Bison	red skin, round	good	good	n/suit	good
Chieftain	red skin	good	good	good	good
Desiree	red skin, yellow flesh	good	good	good	good
Irish Cobbler	white skin	good	good	good	good
Katahdin	white skin, flat	good	good	good	fair
Kennebec	white skin, uneven, large	good	good	good	fair
Norland	red skin, oval	good	good	good	good
Red Pontiac	red skin, round	good	good	good	good
Russet Burbank	russet color, white flesh	good	good	excel	fair
Sebago	white skin, oval	good	good	excel	good
Sequoia	white skin, round	good	fair	n/suit	good
Superior	white skin	good	good	good	good
Yukon Gold	gold flesh	good	excel	good	good

Bison — good for frying, baking and mashing, but not French fries.

Chieftain — a good all-purpose red-skinned potato.

Desiree — a yellow-fleshed type, excellent for baking, frying, boiling and mashing.

Irish Cobbler — an old standby with good flavor.

Katahdin — white-skinned type, suitable for general cooking and frying.

Kennebec — excellent for frying and boiling.

Norland — high-quality all-rounder.

Pontiac — red-skinned type; one of the best for mashing and boiling.

Russet Burbank — a long, white-skinned type developed in the United States; the best potato for frying, used by McDonald's throughout the world for its French fries.

Sebago — white-skinned type, used for French fries, mashing and baking.

Sequoia — common variety of new potato, ideal for boiling.

Superior — all purpose, good shape-keeping quality.

Yukon Gold — a wonderful baking potato with gold flesh.

Nomenclature can be confusing, as it varies from country to country and sometimes represents variety, sometimes place of origin. Many experts would like to see potatoes reclassified, according to such things as starch content.

Buying and Storing

When buying potatoes it is important to choose firm, dry potatoes with unbroken skins that are free from sprouts and green patches. Uneven surfaces and eyes cause no real harm. They simply make preparation time longer.

Green spots on potatoes result from exposure to light. The green color indicates the presence of chlorophyll which could mean the existence of solanine, a toxin which has been known to cause illness. The green patches, which give the potato a bitter taste, can be cut out if they appear only in small patches. Otherwise, the potato should be discarded.

The best way to store potatoes is unwashed (and dry) in a dark, cool, dry place. They should never be refrigerated (except for new potatoes). Store them away from onions, which speed up their spoilage. Once potatoes begin to sprout, show green patches or go soft, they should be discarded.

New potatoes do not keep as well as the other varieties, and should be bought only in small quantities. They are at their best when the skin has a ragged appearance, and feels slightly moist.

Few people are aware that potatoes can be frozen for up to three months. Peel, wash and slice potatoes; plunge into boiling water for two minutes, rinse thoroughly in cold water, dry and pack into plastic bags to freeze.

HANDY HINT
Keep water used to cook vegetables in refrigerator and use to make stock. Vegetable water sealed or covered will keep in the refrigerator for 6 days, or frozen for 3 months.

Cooking Techniques

Careful preparation can make all the difference to the way your potatoes look and taste. Remove all green patches, bruises, eyes and any other marks. Peel potatoes evenly but not too deeply, as vitamins and minerals are stored in and just below the skin.

When dicing or slicing, make potato pieces the same size: this insures even cooking and equal cooking time. To prepare perfect French fries, see pages 66–67.

Boiling: This takes approximately 40 minutes (whole), 20 minutes (quartered), 12 minutes (diced). Cook potatoes in only a small quantity of boiling water, to avoid loss of nutrients. Cooking water can be kept to make a vitamin-rich soup or casserole. More vitamins and minerals are retained if you boil potatoes in their skins.

Baking: Potatoes can be placed directly on a rack in the oven or in a baking dish with a little oil or butter. This method takes approximately one hour at 400°F (200°C), and is another good way of retaining nutrients.

Oven Steaming: Pour a small amount of water into a pan, place potatoes on a rack over the water, and cover. This method takes about one hour at 400°F (200°C).

Pressure Cooking: This is an excellent way to retain color and nutrients, and takes about one-third of the time it takes to boil potatoes.

Steaming: This method also preserves color and nutrients but takes slightly longer than boiling. Place a small amount of boiling water in a pan, and arrange potatoes in a perforated container over the water. Time varies with size of potato, and whether you steam whole or quartered. If quartering, parboil briefly first, so potatoes don't break.

POMMES
Spaniards often refer to potatoes as pommes or 'apples of love' due to the supposed aphrodisiac qualities.

Peel thinly, as vitamins are stored in and just below the skin.

Dice potatoes into the same size pieces for even cooking.

Stewing and in Casseroles: Potatoes should be placed with other vegetables or meat in a covered dish and cooked on the stove top, or in the oven at 350°F (180°C) for about one hour.

Frying: Pan-frying is a great way to cook leftovers. The potatoes should be cooked in 1 inch (2.5 cm) of oil.

Leftovers or thinly sliced potatoes can also be pan-fried in one tbsp (15 mL) of oil or butter, and deep-frying gives us French fries, increasingly popular in fast food chains throughout the world.

Microwaving: This is the most nutritious way to cook potatoes. If cooking them in their skins, prick

them first to prevent them exploding from the build-up of steam and heated juices. When cooking more than one potato at a time, arrange them in a circle on a paper towel or in a microwave-safe dish, and rearrange from time to time to ensure even cooking. Choose similar-sized potatoes so they take the same amount of time to cook.

Slice potatoes the same thickness to ensure even cooking.

As every microwave oven is slightly different, and wattages can vary considerably, cooking times will also vary. Times given in our recipes are based on a 600 watt oven, so if your oven wattage is lower, increase cooking time slightly; if your wattage is higher, decrease cooking time slightly. Always undercook, test for taste and doneness, and if necessary, return to the oven briefly.

To boil potatoes in your microwave, scrub new potatoes and prick with a fork, but do not peel. Place in a shallow dish with 2 tbsp (30 mL) of water. Old potatoes should be peeled, cut into quarters or slices, and placed in a dish with 4 tbsp (60 mL) of water and a pinch of salt. Cover dishes with plastic wrap, rolled back at one edge. Stir once during cooking. Microwave on HIGH (100%) until tender. Leave new potatoes to stand 5 minutes and old potatoes for 3 minutes.

To stuff potatoes, scoop out cooked flesh and leave a 1 inch (2.5 cm) border.

POTATO COOKING TECHNIQUES

METHOD	TIME	TECHNIQUE
Boil	40 minutes (whole) 20 minutes (quartered) 12 minutes (diced)	Scrub well, peel if desired, and use only a small amount of boiling water for new potatoes, cold water for old. Add salt, if preferred, and cover.
Roast	40–60 minutes	Peel, halve or quarter and arrange in a baking dish with a little oil or butter. Cook at 475°F (250°C).
Foil bake	40–60 minutes	Wash well, rub skins well with a little oil, wrap in foil and bake at 475°F (250°C).
French fry	18 minutes minimum	Slice potatoes into strips, chill in a bowl of ice water 10 minutes minimum; drain. Heat deep-frying oil to 375°F (190°C), cook fries in a basket 5–8 minutes; drain. Raise oil temperature to 400°F (200°C), cook fries again, 3–5 minutes; drain well.
Bake	40–60 minutes	Wash well, and place on a rack in the oven; bake at 400°F (200°C).
Mash	15 minutes	Wash, peel and dice; boil until just tender. Drain well and mash with butter, milk, salt and pepper, to taste.
Dry mash	15 minutes	Wash, peel and dice; boil until just tender and mash.
Microwave	1 minute per small potato + 2 minutes standing time	To boil small new potatoes in skins: prick first, place in a dish with 2 tbsp (30 mL) water, cover and microwave on HIGH (100%).
	6 minutes + 3–5 minutes standing time	To boil peeled and diced: place in a dish with 1 tbsp (15 mL) water and a dash salt, cover with plastic wrap leaving one corner turned back, stir once during cooking and microwave on high (100%).
Steam	15 minutes minimum	Place a small amount of water in a pan, arrange potatoes in a steamer over water, cover and cook 15 minutes (diced), 25 minutes (quartered), or 50 minutes (whole).
Oven steam	1 hour	Place small amount of water in a pan, arrange potatoes on a rack over water, cover and cook.

Perfect Potatoes

There are so many ways to make perfect potatoes, but all involve a few basic techniques. Once mastered, you can branch out and experiment with endless variations of your own.

On these two pages, you will find reliable recipes for some classic potato dishes: roasted, mashed, baked in foil and served with sour cream, potato cups and herbed potatoes with parsley and butter. These favorites can accompany almost any dish or make a snack on their own.

HERBED POTATOES

2 small new potatoes per person, lightly scrubbed
1 tsp (5 mL) butter per 2 potatoes
2 tsp (10 mL) chopped fresh parsley or basil, per 2 potatoes

Place potatoes in a pan and just cover with boiling water. Bring to a boil and simmer until tender, approximately 20 minutes. (Alternatively prick potatoes with a fork, crowd into a small dish, cover with a lid or plastic wrap and microwave on HIGH, allowing 1 minute per potato. Let stand 2 minutes.)

Drain. Melt butter in a pan, add parsley and potatoes, and coat potatoes well with parsley butter (or microwave butter with parsley on HIGH 1 minute. Remove from microwave, add potatoes and shake well to cover). Serve immediately.

TASTY VARIATION:
☐ Use 2 tsp (10 mL) per person of any chopped fresh herbs or a sprinkle of freshly ground black pepper, to taste.

BEST ROAST POTATOES

6 medium potatoes, peeled
3 tbsp (45 mL) oil

Wash potatoes and let stand in cold water for 30 minutes. Pat dry with paper towels. Cut potatoes in half lengthwise.

Heat oil in a baking dish for 5 minutes. Add potatoes and bake at 475°F (250°C) for 20 minutes. Turn potatoes over. Bake 20 minutes more or until golden. Drain on paper towels to absorb excess oil. Serve immediately.

Serves 6

BAKED IDAHO POTATOES

oil
6 large new potatoes, washed and dried

TO SERVE
½ cup (125 mL) sour cream, plain yogurt or cottage cheese
3 tbsp (45 mL) freshly chopped chives or fresh parsley, or
1 slice bacon, finely diced or shredded

Rub a little oil over each potato and wrap in a square of aluminum foil.

Arrange on a baking tray and bake at 475°F (250°C) for 40 minutes or until tender (or wrap potatoes in microwave-proof plastic wrap and microwave on HIGH 10–12 minutes; let stand 2 minutes).

Remove foil or plastic wrap and cut a criss-cross pattern across the top of each potato. Gently squeeze potato until the top opens. Serve with a dollop of sour cream, yogurt or cottage cheese and top with chives, bacon or parsley.

Serves 6

POTATO CUPS

These are great served with a salad, as a light snack or as an accompaniment for barbecues, buffets and even a special dinner party. Allow 1–2 potatoes per person.

medium old potatoes
oil

Scrub the skins to remove dirt and prick with a skewer several times. Place potatoes well apart on a rack and bake at 350°F (180°C) for 1 hour or until tender (or microwave on HIGH 10 minutes). Let cool.

When potatoes are cool enough to handle, cut in half and scoop out the pulp, leaving a ½ inch (1 cm) thick shell. Mash the potato pulp and set aside to use in filling of your choice (see Fillings recipes).

Brush potatoes inside and out with oil and arrange on a greased oven tray, cut side up. Bake at 400°F (200°C) for 10 minutes. (Microwaving will not make the skins crisp.)

Potatoes are now ready for filling.

HEALTHY FILLING

6 Potato Cups (see recipe)
5 tbsp (75 mL) plain yogurt or cottage cheese
1 tbsp (15 mL) chopped fresh parsley or mint

Combine yogurt or cottage cheese and parsley or mint. Spoon into shells and heat.

Fills 6 potatoes.

SIZE OF POTATOES
Most of the recipes in our book specify what size potato to use. Those that don't leave it to your discretion. In general, the following sizes may be useful:

large 7 oz (200 g)
medium 5 oz (150 g)
small 3½ oz (100 g)

MASHED
If mashing, allow 1½ medium-sized potatoes per person, or 2–3 new potatoes, depending on size, if serving whole.

BAKING POTATOES WITH ROASTS
When cooking baked potatoes with a roast, don't place potatoes under the meat as the juices will soften the potatoes and they will not get crisp. Arrange around the meat or cook in a separate dish in the oven.

Potatoes make ideal accompaniments. Try Herbed Potatoes, Best Roast Potatoes, Baked Idaho Potatoes and Potato Cups with Healthy Filling.

The Country Trader

Chelsea House Antiques

Tasty Beginnings

Soups and starters make fabulous first courses, light meals or tempting snacks. In the following selection, you can also find ideal party food, easy to hand around on trays or arrange as a buffet.

TARAMOSALATA

4 thick slices white bread
warm water
1 medium potato, peeled, cooked and
**   dry mashed**
½ cup (125 mL) tarama (see Glossary)
1 clove garlic, crushed
½ small onion, peeled and grated
1 egg, separated
¼ cup (60 mL) lemon juice
¼ – ½ cup (60 – 125 mL) olive oil
black olives and crusty French bread,
**   to serve**

Cut crusts from bread slices, put bread in a bowl and cover with warm water for 3 minutes. Drain and gently squeeze bread to remove water.

In a blender or food processor, combine potato, tarama, garlic and onion. Blend until smooth. Gradually add egg yolk, lemon juice and sufficient oil to make a thick, smooth sauce. If beating by hand, add egg white to the mixture and beat very well with a spoon.

Spoon mixture into a serving bowl and chill thoroughly. Serve accompanied by olives and crusty bread.

Serves 6

TASTY VARIATION:
☐ Taramosalata also goes well with Cucumber Dip (see recipe) served in separate bowls; or with raw vegetables, such as cucumber and celery sticks, radishes, sliced mushrooms and cauliflower florets.

CUCUMBER DIP

1 cup (250 mL) plain yogurt
1 cucumber, peeled and grated
1 clove garlic, crushed
1 green onion, finely diced

Combine all ingredients and chill thoroughly in a serving bowl.

Serves 4–6.

DEEP-FRIED VEGETABLES WITH TOMATO DIP

BATTER
1 cup (250 mL) chickpea flour
**   or self-rising flour (see Glossary)**
½ tsp (2.5 mL) chili powder
½ tsp (2.5 mL) baking soda
water, to mix

TOMATO DIP
1 cup (250 mL) puréed tomatoes
1¼ cups (310 mL) plain yogurt
¼ tsp (1 mL) ground cumin
1 tbsp (15 mL) chopped fresh parsley

VEGETABLES
1 potato, peeled and sliced
1 eggplant, peeled and thinly sliced
1 onion, sliced
1 green pepper, seeded and sliced
4 cauliflower florets
oil for deep-frying

To make the batter, combine flour, chili powder and baking soda. Whisk in sufficient water to make a smooth batter.

To make the tomato dip, combine all the dip ingredients in a serving bowl.

Dip all the vegetables into batter. Fry in hot oil until golden brown and drain on paper towels. To serve, arrange fried vegetables on a platter with the tomato dip.

Serves 6

Deep-fried Vegetables with Tomato Dip, Taramosalata and Cucumber Dip

POTATO STICKS

1 large potato, peeled and cooked
2 egg yolks
3 tbsp (45 mL) butter
1 cup (250 mL) self-rising flour
pepper to taste
1 tbsp (15 mL) chopped fresh chives
1 egg, beaten
sesame seeds, to garnish

Mash potato with egg yolks and butter until creamy. Beat in flour, pepper and chives to form a dough. Chill for 1 hour.

On a floured board, roll out dough to ½ inch (1 cm) thick. Cut into strips 2½ inches (6 cm) long, ½ inch (1 cm) wide. Twist, brush lightly with beaten egg and sprinkle with sesame seeds. Bake for 10 minutes at 400°F (200°C) until crisp and brown. Cool and serve as appetizers.

TASTY VARIATION:
☐ Instead of sesame seeds, use grated cheese or caraway seeds, to taste.

Serves 2

FETTUCCINE WITH POTATO AND TOMATO SAUCE

1 lb (450 g) fettuccine, cooked

SAUCE
1½ tbsp (20 mL) butter
2 green onions, diced
2 celery stalks, diced
½ green pepper, diced
1 zucchini, diced
1 large potato, peeled and diced
4 slices bacon, diced
1¾ cups (440 mL) canned tomatoes with liquid
1 cup (250 mL) water
1 cube chicken stock
pinch dried thyme
1 clove garlic, crushed

Melt butter, add all vegetables (except tomatoes) and bacon and gently fry until bacon fat becomes clear. Add all remaining ingredients. Bring to a boil and simmer for 30 minutes. (Alternatively, microwave butter, green onions and bacon on HIGH 2 minutes. Add diced potato and cook 2 minutes. Add remaining ingredients and microwave on HIGH 10 minutes). Serve with cooked fettuccine.

Serves 6

Fettuccine with Potato and Tomato Sauce

BAKED OR FRIED POTATO SKINS WITH AIOLI SAUCE DIP

Yes! even the humble potato skin can be used — and with scrumptious results.

6 medium potatoes
3 tbsp (45 mL) melted butter (for baked skins)
coarse salt
oil for deep-frying (for fried skins)

AIOLI SAUCE DIP
cooked pulp of 2 medium potatoes
8 cloves garlic, crushed
1 cup (250 mL) virgin olive oil
1 egg yolk
1 tsp (5 mL) lemon juice

Scrub potatoes, rinse well and pat dry. Pierce the skins several times with a fork. Bake in a 350°F (180°C) oven for 45–60 minutes or until tender (or microwave on HIGH 8 minutes, let stand 4 minutes). Cool slightly, cut in half and scoop out flesh, leaving a ½ inch (1 cm) thick shell. Put aside pulp from 2 of the potatoes to use in the Aioli Sauce Dip. Using a sharp knife, cut each shell lengthwise into eight equal sections.

For baked skins, brush inside and out with melted butter and sprinkle with coarse salt. Place on a baking sheet and bake in a 475°F (250°C) oven for 10–12 minutes until crisp.

For fried skins, heat oil and fry skins until crisp. Drain on paper towels.

To prepare the sauce, combine potato pulp, garlic and half the oil in a blender. Blend till smooth. Add egg yolk and slowly add remaining oil and the lemon juice. To make the sauce without a blender, mash potato, add garlic and beat in one-quarter of the oil, all the egg yolk and lemon juice. Slowly beat in remaining oil. This method will take about 10 minutes. If sauce is too thick, add 2 tsp (10 mL) hot water. Serve sauce in a dip bowl surrounded by potato skins.

Serves 6

TASTY VARIATIONS:
Replace Aioli Sauce Dip with:
☐ 1 cup (250 mL) sour cream mixed with 3 tbsp (45 mL) chopped fresh chives; or
☐ 1 cup (250 g) cottage cheese with 2 ounces (60 g) diced smoked salmon.

CRUSHING GINGER
For a time-saving trick, use a garlic press to crush fresh ginger.

Avocado Bake

AVOCADO BAKE

6 medium potatoes, washed and dried
3 tbsp (45 mL) butter
2 ripe avocados, peeled and sliced
1 tbsp (15 mL) lemon juice

FILLING
3 tbsp (45 mL) butter
1 tbsp (15 mL) flour
1 tsp (5 mL) powdered chicken stock
1 tsp (5 mL) curry powder
1 cup (250 mL) milk
8 oz (225 g) canned salmon or tuna,
  drained and bones removed

Bake potatoes in a 350°F (180°C) oven for 1 hour (or microwave on HIGH 8 minutes, let stand for 4 minutes). Remove from oven or microwave and cool. Cut one-third from the top of each potato and scoop out potato pulp, leaving ½ inch (1 cm) thick shell.

Melt 3 tbsp (45 mL) butter in a saucepan (or microwave on HIGH 30 seconds) and brush over the outside of potato shells. Bake shells in a 350°F (180°C) oven for 15 minutes. This step must be done in a conventional oven.

While shells are baking, prepare filling. Melt 3 tbsp (45 mL) butter in a saucepan and stir in flour, chicken stock and curry powder. Stir for 1 minute over medium heat, making sure there are no lumps. Remove from heat and stir in milk. Return to heat, stirring until mixture boils and thickens. Add fish.

(Alternatively, microwave butter on HIGH 30 seconds. Stir in flour, chicken stock, curry powder and microwave on HIGH 1 minute. Beat in milk. Microwave on HIGH 2 minutes or until mixture boils and thickens. Stir well, then add fish.)

Fill the potato shells with salmon mixture and top with avocado slices sprinkled with lemon juice to prevent browning. Return to 350°F (180°C) oven for 15 minutes to heat through (or microwave on HIGH 2 – 4 minutes).

Serves 6

TASTY VARIATION:
☐ Sprinkle grated cheese over the top and brown under broiler or in oven before serving.

LEMON JUICE
Always sprinkle fruits, such as avocados, bananas and apples, with lemon juice to prevent browning. Prepare as close to serving time as possible and the fruit will look luscious when it reaches the table.

Chilled soups are delightful served for an al fresco summer lunch or dinner.

CURRIED POTATO SOUP

This soup tastes especially good served with parsley sprigs set in ice cubes.

3 tbsp (45 mL) butter
3 onions, sliced
6 medium potatoes, peeled and sliced
1 tbsp (15 mL) curry powder
2 cubes chicken stock
1 tbsp (15 mL) tamarind sauce
(see *Note*)
2 cups (500 mL) water
6 ice cubes with parsley sprigs set in
them (optional)

Melt butter, add onions and gently fry till transparent. Add potatoes, curry powder, crumbled stock cubes, tamarind sauce and cover with water. Bring to a boil and simmer for 30 minutes. Blend or push through a sieve. Chill thoroughly before serving.

Serves 4

Note: Tamarind sauce can be replaced by 1 tbsp (15 mL) lemon juice.

GREEN HERB SOUP

1½ tbsp (20 mL) butter
6 green onions, whites and greens
sliced
1 large potato, peeled and diced
4 outer lettuce leaves, washed and
torn into small pieces
2 cups (500 mL) water
juice of ½ lemon
pepper to taste
3 tbsp (45 mL) chopped fresh herbs
(see *Note*)
½ cup (125 mL) cream

Melt butter, add green onions and fry over low heat until tender (or microwave butter and green onions together on HIGH 1 minute). Add diced potato and stir for 1 minute (or microwave on HIGH 30 seconds, then place in a pan). Add lettuce to the pan. Cover with water and bring to a boil. Simmer for 20 minutes. Stir in lemon juice and pepper, then, if using a blender, add herbs and blend until smooth. Or push soup through a sieve, then add herbs. Add cream and chill.

Serves 6

Note: Use any fresh herbs, or a mixture of herbs: basil, parsley, mint, thyme, rosemary, sage, sorrel.

Curried Potato Soup and Green Herb Soup

CUCUMBER AND LIME SOUP

1 large cucumber, peeled, seeded and sliced
3 medium potatoes, peeled and sliced
2 green onions, diced
1 cup (250 mL) water
juice of 3 limes
½ cup (125 mL) cream
cucumber or lime twists, to garnish

Combine cucumber, potatoes, green onions, water and lime juice in a pan. Bring to a boil and simmer for 30 minutes. Blend till smooth or push through a sieve. Stir in cream and chill thoroughly. Serve in six wide champagne glasses with a twist of cucumber or lime.

Serves 6

SATAY SAUCE

1½ tbsp (20 mL) butter
1 medium onion, peeled and diced
½ tsp (2.5 mL) chili powder
pepper to taste
¼ cup (60 mL) sugar
5 tbsp (75 mL) peanut butter
¼ cup (60 mL) white vinegar
2 tsp (10 mL) soy sauce
1 cup (250 mL) water

Over low heat, melt butter in a pan, add onion and fry till tender. Add remaining ingredients, simmer for 10–12 minutes or until thick, then serve.

(Or combine butter and onion and microwave on HIGH 2 minutes. Add remaining ingredients and microwave on HIGH 2 minutes or until mixture thickens.)

This sauce will keep refrigerated in a covered jar for up to two weeks.

Makes approximately 1¼ cups (310 mL).

SPICY POTATO PUFFS

5 tbsp (75 mL) vegetable oil
1 clove garlic, crushed
1 medium onion, peeled and sliced
1 tbsp (15 mL) chopped fresh coriander leaves
1 tbsp (15 mL) ground turmeric
pepper to taste
1 tbsp (15 mL) sugar
1 lb (450 g) ground chicken or pork
1 large potato, cooked and dry mashed
1 green onion, finely diced
2 lbs (1 kg) prepared puff pastry
oil for deep-frying
Satay Sauce, store-bought or homemade (see recipe), to serve

Spicy Potato Puffs are easy to make: mix up filling ingredients, roll dough into circles, spoon on filling and fold dough, pinching edges together to form a decorative edge.

> **POTATO PULP**
> Potato pulp can be covered or put in an airtight container and stored in the refrigerator for three days.

Heat oil in a wok or frying pan. Fry garlic until golden brown. Add onion, coriander and turmeric and stir for 1 minute. Add pepper, sugar and ground chicken. Stir until meat has browned. Stir in mashed potato and green onion, then remove from heat. Allow to cool.

Cut each pastry sheet into four 4 inch (10 cm) squares. In the center of each square, place a spoonful of the mixture. Fold pastry into a triangle, pinching edges together with your fingers to form a curly edge. Place each triangle on a sheet of waxed paper dusted with flour. Repeat until all the pastry and filling are used. Refrigerate until ready to use.

Heat oil for deep-frying. When hot, fry each triangle until golden brown then drain. Set aside in a warm oven while frying the remaining puffs, a few at a time. Serve with Satay Sauce (see recipe).

Makes approximately 24 triangles.

Handy hint: Make the puffs in advance and freeze them uncooked. To use, thaw then fry.

TASTY VARIATION:
☐ Use 1 lb (450 g) of any leftover meat, ground chicken, lamb or beef.

> **ICE CUBES**
> For a professional touch, serve chilled summer soups with ice cubes set with a sprig of fresh parsley or another favorite herb fresh from your garden.

SEAFOOD IN A BASKET

1 lb (450 g) uncooked shrimp, shelled and deveined
1 lb (450 g) fish fillets, cut in 1 inch (2.5 cm) pieces
3 tbsp (45 mL) lemon juice
½ lb (225 g) scallops
3 tbsp (45 mL) milk
3 tbsp (45 mL) oil
½ tsp (2.5 mL) sesame oil
½ lb (225 g) snow peas, topped and tailed
3 tbsp (45 mL) Hoisin sauce (see Note)

POTATO BASKETS
6 large potatoes, peeled and coarsely grated
3 tbsp (45 mL) cornstarch
oil for deep-frying

Cut shrimp in half lengthwise. Combine shrimp and fish in a bowl and pour lemon juice over them. Put scallops in another bowl and cover with milk. Allow both to marinate while you make the baskets.

Pat grated potatoes dry with paper towels. In a bowl combine potatoes with cornstarch. Lightly oil a medium and small strainer. Place one-sixth of the potato mixture in the medium strainer. Press the small strainer onto the potato to form the shape of a cup. Heat oil until very hot. Holding both strainer handles tightly, lower the strainers into the hot oil. Cook until the potato is golden and tap out onto a baking sheet. Repeat until you have six baskets. Keep the baskets hot in a 350°F (180°C) oven while cooking the seafood.

Heat both the oils in a wok or frying pan, add the drained seafood and stir-fry for 2 minutes. Add snow peas and Hoisin sauce. Stir-fry 30 seconds more. To serve, position a potato basket on each plate and fill with seafood mix.

Serves 6

Note: Similar in appearance to barbecue sauce, Hoisin sauce is a thick red spicy sauce made from soybeans, garlic and onion. Available from supermarkets and delicatessens, it is used to flavor vegetables, shellfish and duck.

TASTY VARIATIONS:
☐ Replace Hoisin sauce with 1–3 tbsp (15–45 mL) soy sauce.
☐ For an extra nutty flavor, fry 2 tbsp (20 g) almond halves with the snow peas.

1. Combine potatoes and cornstarch.

2. Place one-sixth of mixture in medium strainer.

3. Press small strainer into potato to form
   a cup shape.

4. Holding handles tightly,
   lower strainers into hot oil.

5. To serve, fill each potato
   basket with seafood mixture.

Crab Mornay

CREAMY SCALLOP SOUP

½ lb (225 g) scallops
1 cup (250 mL) milk
1 lb (450 g) fish fillets
4 cups (1 L) water
1 cup (250 mL) white wine
3 tbsp (45 mL) butter
1 onion, sliced
2 medium potatoes, peeled and sliced
2 egg yolks beaten with ¼ cup
(60 mL) cream
crusty bread, to serve

Trim the orange roe from the scallops and set aside. Dice the white part and cover with milk in a bowl. Arrange fish in a frying pan with water and wine. Bring to a boil, lower heat and simmer for 30 minutes. Remove fish, flake, discard bones and set fish aside. Reserve cooking liquid.

Melt butter in a pan and lightly fry onion; add sliced potatoes and fish cooking liquid. Bring to a boil, lower heat and simmer 30 minutes.

In another pan, simmer scallops and milk without boiling for 4 minutes only.

In a blender, place flaked fish, scallops and milk, onions, potatoes and fish cooking liquid. Blend, then stir in combined egg yolks and cream.

To serve, reheat without boiling, stirring all the time (or microwave on HIGH until soup starts to steam). Serve in a tureen or in soup bowls, with crusty bread.

Serves 8

CRAB MORNAY

3 tbsp (45 mL) butter
4 green onions, chopped
1 tbsp (15 mL) flour
½ cup (125 mL) milk
¼ cup (60 mL) white wine
2 tsp (10 mL) Dijon mustard
1 lb (450 g) canned red crabmeat,
drained
½ cup (125 mL) cream

TOPPING
4 medium potatoes, peeled and
cooked
dash milk and butter, for mashing
grated cheese, to taste
6 slices lemon and chopped fresh
parsley, to serve

Melt butter in a pan and fry green onions until tender. Add flour and cook for 1 minute, stirring continually. Remove from heat, stir in milk, wine and Dijon mustard. Return to heat and bring to a boil, stirring constantly. Add crabmeat and cream.

(Alternatively, combine butter and green onions and microwave on HIGH 2 minutes. Stir in flour and microwave on HIGH 1 minute. Stir in milk, wine and mustard and microwave on HIGH 2 minutes. Stir well and add crabmeat and cream.)

Spoon mixture into six individual gratin dishes, or serve in a large baking dish.

To make the topping, mash cooked potatoes with milk and butter. Spread over crab mixture and sprinkle with grated cheese. Brown under broiler (or microwave on HIGH until cheese melts). Garnish with lemon slices and parsley.

Serves 6

TASTY VARIATION:
☐ Replace crabmeat with 1 lb (450 g) of any seafood, freshly cooked or canned.

SEAFOOD
Never boil seafood – it becomes tough. Follow recipe instructions carefully: they may specify boiling shrimp shells or heads, for example; seafood flesh, such as shrimp meat or scallops, should be simmered gently on low heat.

VICHYSSOISE

2 leeks
ice water
3 tbsp (45 mL) butter
2 large potatoes, peeled and sliced
2 chicken stock cubes
2 cups (500 mL) water
1¼ cups (310 mL) cream

Slice the white part of the leeks and finely shred the tender parts of the green tops. Cover the green tops with ice water (to make them curl).

Melt butter, add white part of leeks and fry until soft (or microwave on HIGH 2 minutes). Add potatoes, stock cubes and water, and bring to a boil. Lower heat and simmer for 30 minutes. Blend soup until smooth or push through a sieve. Stir in cream and chill thoroughly. Serve in six glass bowls garnished with the curly leek tops.

Serves 6

SCAMPI OR SHRIMP IN GARLIC SAUCE

4 medium potatoes, peeled and cooked
2 egg yolks
¼ cup (60 mL) milk
1½ tbsp (20 mL) butter

GARLIC SAUCE
12 uncooked scampi or 24 uncooked shrimp
1 cup (250 mL) white wine
3 tbsp (45 mL) butter
1 small onion, peeled and sliced
2 cloves garlic, crushed
1 tbsp (15 mL) flour
½ cup (125 mL) milk
½ cup (125 mL) cream
1 tbsp (15 mL) chopped fresh parsley

Mash potatoes with egg yolks, milk and 1½ tbsp (20 mL) butter to a creamy texture.

Lightly butter six ovenproof dinner plates. Put a spoonful of potato mixture on each plate and, using a fork, make a nest. Place plates in 350°F (180°C) oven. (Alternatively, spoon potato mixture on to plates and microwave on HIGH 2 minutes.)

To prepare sauce, break off the shrimp heads, remove the shells and devein. Combine heads and wine in a saucepan and bring to a boil. Boil until liquid is reduced by one-third. Strain, reserving liquid.

Melt 3 tbsp (45 mL) butter in a saucepan, add onion and gently fry until tender, but not brown. Add garlic, stir in flour and cook for 1 minute, making sure there are no lumps. Remove from heat. Stir in milk and reserved wine. Return to heat and, stirring constantly, bring mixture to a boil and allow to thicken. Add shrimp, carefully stirring, and cook until shrimp turn a pale pink. Do not allow mixture to boil. Gently stir in cream and parsley. Heat without boiling.

(Alternatively, combine 3 tbsp (45 mL) butter, the onion and garlic and microwave on HIGH 1 minute. Add flour and cook on HIGH 1 minute. Gradually add wine and milk, stirring until smooth, and microwave on HIGH 2 minutes or until mixture boils and thickens. Stir well. Add shrimp, cream and parsley and microwave on MEDIUM 1 minute.)

To serve, remove plates from oven or microwave and, with a slotted spoon, divide shrimp into each nest. Carefully spoon sauce over shrimp.

Serves 6

Note: Scampi are very large shrimp, originally from the Adriatic Sea and much used in Italian cooking. If unavailable, substitute any large shrimp.

Shrimp in Beer Batter

SHRIMP IN BEER BATTER

2 large potatoes, cooked and mashed with cream
18 uncooked shrimp
1 cup (250 mL) flour
6 oz (180 mL) beer
oil for deep-frying

SAUCE
3 slices fresh or canned pineapple, finely chopped
1 cup (250 mL) mayonnaise
2 tsp (10 mL) curry powder

Spoon mashed potatoes into an ovenproof bowl. Warm in 350°F (180°C) oven (or microwave on HIGH 2 minutes just before serving).

Shell shrimp, leaving their tails on, and devein. Combine flour and beer in a bowl and mix to a smooth batter. If the mixture is too thick, stir in a little water.

Heat the oil. Holding a shrimp by the tail, dip it into the batter then carefully fry a few at a time until golden brown. Remove and drain on paper towels. Repeat until all shrimp are cooked.

To make the sauce, combine pineapple, mayonnaise and curry powder in a bowl. Divide between six small bowls, arranged in the center of six dinner plates.

To serve, spoon the hot mashed potato around the sauce bowls. Position three shrimp on each potato bed with the tails pointing outward.

Or spoon potato into bowls, arrange shrimp decoratively on top and serve sauce separately.

Serves 6

TASTY VARIATION:
☐ For a tropical touch, after the shrimp have been dipped in batter, roll in shredded coconut and then fry.

Sensational Salads

Delicious meals that are good for you as well – these recipes are perfect for festive summer lunches or light family meals with a difference. Combine potatoes with a variety of ingredients, such as chicken, seafood, crispy vegetables and fresh fruit, pour over a favorite dressing and you have an easy-to-prepare dish for the whole family.

DILL-MUSTARD POTATO SALAD

8 cups (2 L) chicken stock
2 lbs (1 kg) new baby potatoes, unpeeled and scrubbed
¾ cup (180 mL) vegetable oil
1 egg, room temperature
¼ cup (60 mL) Dijon mustard
3 tbsp (45 mL) finely chopped fresh dill or 2 tsp (10 mL) dried
1 tsp (5 mL) red wine vinegar
1 tsp (5 mL) lemon juice
freshly ground black pepper
½ cup (125 mL) sour cream
3 celery stalks, thinly sliced
1 onion, thinly sliced
chopped chives, to garnish

Combine stock and potatoes and bring to a boil over high heat. Reduce heat and cook potatoes just until tender. Drain immediately and rinse with cold water to cool. Drain potatoes well.

In a food processor or blender combine ¼ cup (60 mL) oil with the egg, mustard, dill, vinegar, lemon juice and pepper and blend until mixture is slightly thickened, about 10 seconds. With machine running, slowly pour in remaining oil in a thin, steady stream. Mix well. Add sour cream and blend 3 seconds to combine.

Slice potatoes into quarters and arrange in a salad bowl with celery and onion. Pour in the dressing and fold through the salad. Cover and refrigerate until ready to serve. Garnish with chives.

Serves 6

POTATO SALAD WITH PESTO MAYONNAISE

3 lbs (1.5 kg) small new potatoes
salt
¼ cup (60 mL) pine nuts
fresh basil leaves

PESTO MAYONNAISE
3 egg yolks
1 tsp (5 mL) Dijon mustard
1 tbsp (15 mL) white wine vinegar
3 cloves garlic, peeled
1½ cups (375 mL) olive oil
salt and pepper to taste
½ cup (125 mL) chopped fresh basil
¼ cup (60 mL) fresh parsley
¼ cup (60 mL) grated Parmesan cheese

Wash and scrub potatoes if necessary. Cook in boiling salted water until just tender, about 20 minutes depending on their size. Drain and cool.

To make Pesto Mayonnaise, place egg yolks in blender or food processor with mustard, vinegar and garlic. Blend until smooth. Still blending, add the oil in a slow steady stream, until a thick mayonnaise has formed. Season well with salt and pepper. Add basil and parsley and blend until smooth. Add Parmesan cheese and blend until combined.

Fold mayonnaise through warm potatoes and spoon into a serving bowl. Lightly toast pine nuts in a dry frying pan and sprinkle over the potato salad. Decorate with fresh basil leaves.

Serves 4–6

Potato Salad with Pesto Mayonnaise, Sliced Potatoes Vinaigrette, and Dill-Mustard Potato Salad

BASIC POTATO SALAD

8 cups (2 L) chicken stock
2 lbs (1 kg) Pontiac potatoes, peeled
¼ cup (60 mL) fresh mint sprigs

DRESSING
1 cup (250 mL) mayonnaise
½ cup (125 mL) sour cream
freshly ground black pepper
½ tsp (2.5 mL) mustard powder

Bring stock to a boil in a large saucepan. Add potatoes and mint and cook for 15 minutes or until just tender. Drain and cool potatoes then cut into ½ inch (1 cm) cubes.

Combine dressing ingredients. Place potatoes in a salad bowl, add dressing and stir. Cover and refrigerate before serving.

Serves 4–6

POTATO SALAD WITH SPICY MAYONNAISE

Basic Potato Salad (see recipe)

SPICY MAYONNAISE
1 cup (250 mL) mayonnaise
½ cup (125 mL) sour cream
freshly ground black pepper
½ tsp (2.5 mL) dry mustard

Combine all the mayonnaise ingredients. Place cooked, cubed potatoes in a salad bowl, add dressing and stir. Cover and refrigerate before serving.

Serves 4–6

SLICED POTATOES VINAIGRETTE

2 lbs (1 kg) red new potatoes, unpeeled

VINAIGRETTE
½ cup (125 mL) finely chopped fresh parsley
5 tbsp (75 mL) freshly snipped chives
¾ cup (180 mL) safflower oil
¼ cup (60 mL) red wine vinegar
2 tsp (10 mL) dry mustard
1 tsp (5 mL) salt
freshly ground pepper

Cook potatoes until a sharp knife slides in easily. (Do not overcook.) Drain and cover with cold water. Let stand 12 minutes and drain again.

Combine parsley and chives in a bowl. Add oil, vinegar and seasonings and whisk to blend.

Slice potatoes into vinaigrette. Invert mixture into serving bowl. Toss gently to coat potatoes evenly, adjust seasoning and serve at room temperature.

Serves 8

Basic Potato Salad
1. Cook potatoes with stock and mint.

2. Drain and cool potatoes in a colander.

3. Cut potatoes into cubes.

4. Combine dressing ingredients in a bowl.

5. Place potatoes in a salad bowl, add dressing and stir gently to combine.

CHICKEN SALAD

1 lb (450 g) cooked chicken, diced
½ fresh pineapple, peeled and diced
2 green onions, diced
1 mandarin orange, broken into
    segments
Basic Potato Salad (see recipe)
¼ cup (60 mL) French Dressing (see
    recipe)
lettuce leaves, washed
2 hard-boiled eggs, shelled and
    chopped
2 tomatoes, sliced
1 stalk celery, diced
¼ cup (60 mL) Tasty Mayonnaise
    (see recipe)
1½ tbsp (20 mL) butter
3 tbsp (45 mL) slivered almonds

In a bowl combine chicken, pineapple, green onions, mandarin segments and potato salad. Add French Dressing and stir.

Place lettuce leaves on a large plate. Spoon chicken salad onto lettuce. Combine eggs, tomatoes, celery and mayonnaise and spoon mixture on top of chicken. Melt butter, add almonds and fry until lightly browned. Sprinkle almonds on top of salad and chill thoroughly.

Serves 6

TASTY VARIATION
☐ Replace chicken with 1 lb (450 g) cooked shrimp, shelled.

CURRIED POTATO SALAD

3 hard-boiled eggs, shelled and sliced
2 stalks celery, diced
1 small green pepper, seeded and
    diced
Basic Potato Salad (see recipe)
1 tbsp (15 mL) curry powder
Tasty Mayonnaise (see recipe)

In a bowl combine eggs, celery, green pepper and potato salad. Mix curry powder with mayonnaise, pour over salad and serve.

Serves 6

FESTIVE POTATO SALAD

8 medium mushrooms, washed and
    diced
⅓ cup (85 mL) French Dressing
    (see recipe)
6 potatoes, peeled, diced and cooked
2 green apples, cored and sliced
juice of 1 lemon
1 orange, peeled and segmented
2 hard-boiled eggs, shelled and sliced
1 carrot, peeled and grated
6 small pickled onions
1 stalk celery, diced
2 tomatoes, sliced
lettuce leaves

Place diced mushrooms in a salad bowl with French Dressing and let stand for at least 2 hours, preferably overnight. Add potatoes to mushrooms and dressing.

Add sliced apples and cover with lemon juice to prevent browning. Add all other ingredients. Chill and serve on lettuce leaves.

Serves 6

JANSSONS TEMPTATION

This is a traditional Swedish recipe. Sweden is home of the smorgasbord – the buffet style of serving where food is not heaped on the plate, but sampled, one or two dishes at a time. This is a very appropriate dish for the casual or formal barbecue.

6 medium potatoes, peeled
2 onions, sliced
10 anchovies, cleaned, or 20 canned
    anchovies
1¾ cups (440 mL) cream
3 tbsp (45 mL) butter

Slice potatoes into strips ½ inch (1 cm) thick. Grease a casserole dish and place one-third of potato strips on bottom. Top with half the onion and half the anchovies. Repeat, finishing with potatoes.

Pour 1¼ cups (310 mL) cream over the potatoes and dot with butter. Bake at 350°F (180°C) for 45 minutes. Before serving, pour remaining cream over potatoes. Serve with any barbecued meat or fish.

Serves 6

TASTY VARIATION
☐ Replace anchovies with 7 oz (200 g) canned tuna, drained.

ITALIAN POTATO SALAD

2 cloves garlic, crushed
½ green pepper, seeded and diced
½ red pepper, seeded and diced
12 black olives
12 green olives
4 slices prosciutto ham cut into strips
1 cup (125 g) diced strong Cheddar
cheese
Basic Potato Salad (see recipe)
Vinaigrette (see recipe)

Combine all salad ingredients in a bowl and chill. Pour vinaigrette over salad and serve.

Serves 6

SALAD NIÇOISE

1 head lettuce, washed
Vinaigrette (see recipe)
4 potatoes, peeled, sliced and cooked
¼ lb (110 g) green beans, sliced and
    cooked
1 onion, finely diced
1 small cucumber, diced
6 tomatoes, quartered
12 black olives
2 hard-boiled eggs, quartered
7 oz (200 g) canned tuna, drained
1 tsp (5 mL) freshly squeezed lemon
    juice
12 anchovy fillets
1 tbsp (15 mL) chopped fresh parsley

Arrange lettuce leaves in a salad bowl. Sprinkle with a little Vinaigrette. Arrange a layer of cold potatoes with beans and onion on top. Sprinkle with dressing. Add a layer of cucumber, tomatoes, olives and eggs. Sprinkle with dressing. Add lemon juice to tuna, break into flakes and add to salad. Decorate top with a lattice effect of anchovy fillets and parsley. Serve chilled (do not allow to stand too long).

Serves 6

CANNED OR FRESH
1 cup (250 mL) canned pineapple pieces or mandarin orange segments may be substituted for fresh.

Salad Niçoise

TASTY MAYONNAISE

3 egg yolks
½ cup (125 mL) virgin olive oil
¼ cup (60 mL) freshly squeezed
  lemon juice
1 tsp (5 mL) sugar
¼ cup (60 mL) cream
1 tbsp (15 mL) Dijon mustard

Beat egg yolks in blender. Gradually beat in oil, lemon juice and sugar and blend on high speed until mixture is smooth. Add cream and mustard, blend 30 seconds, then chill.

If a blender is not used, beat egg yolks, add oil drop by drop, beating well, then add lemon juice, beat again, add sugar, cream and mustard and beat until smooth.

Makes approximately 1¼ cups (310 mL).

FRENCH DRESSING

¼ cup (60 mL) white vinegar
pepper to taste
½ tsp (2.5 mL) sugar
½ tsp (2.5 mL) dry mustard
1 clove garlic, crushed
½ cup (125 mL) virgin olive oil

Blend all ingredients well.

Makes approximately ¾ cup (180 mL).

Handy hint: White wine vinegar may replace white vinegar.

VIRGIN OLIVE OIL
Virgin olive oil is oil taken from the first pressing of the olives, and so tastes especially delicious.

VINAIGRETTE

3 tbsp (45 mL) white vinegar
1 tbsp (15 mL) freshly squeezed
  lemon juice
1 tsp (5 mL) prepared mustard
⅓ cup (85 mL) virgin olive oil

Beat vinegar, lemon juice and mustard together. Add oil, 1 tsp (5 mL) at a time, beating well.

Makes approximately ¾ cup (180 mL).

TASTY VARIATION:
☐ Add 1 tbsp (15 mL) very finely chopped green onions.

BASIC NEW POTATO SALAD

12 new potatoes
1 sprig fresh mint
4 green onions, finely diced
1 tbsp (15 mL) chopped fresh parsley

Wash new potatoes, leaving skins on. Bring to a boil and cook 20 minutes, or until tender (or microwave, covered, in 1 tsp (5 mL) water on HIGH 5–8 minutes, let stand for 2 minutes). Let stand. When cool, slice or dice potatoes into a salad bowl. Add remaining ingredients and chill.

Delicious with Vinaigrette (see recipe), this salad can be served with any dressing you prefer.

Serves 6

GREEK SALAD

½ head romaine, iceberg or curly lettuce
2 radishes, sliced
4 tomatoes, cut into wedges
1 cucumber, sliced
12 black olives
3 oz (90 g) feta cheese
12 anchovy fillets
Basic New Potato Salad (see recipe)

Wash lettuce, shake well and tear into pieces. Use to line a salad bowl. Add all ingredients, crumbling feta cheese, and arrange attractively. Serve with Herb Dressing (see recipe).

Serves 6

HOT POTATO SALAD

2 slices bacon, diced
2 slices bread, diced
¼ cup (60 mL) sour cream
½ cup (125 mL) mayonnaise
2 hard-boiled eggs, shelled and sliced
Basic New Potato Salad (see recipe)
grated strong Cheddar cheese,
to garnish

Fry bacon and bread together until crisp and brown. Drain on paper towels and place in an ovenproof dish. Add all ingredients and sprinkle with cheese. Heat in 350°F (180°C) oven for 15 minutes (or microwave on HIGH 5 minutes). Serve hot with wieners, sausage or barbecued meats.

Serves 6

Hot Potato Salad, Greek Salad, French Vegetable Salad

POTATO NUT SALAD

2 green apples, cored and diced
3 tbsp (45 mL) freshly squeezed
   lemon juice
Basic New Potato Salad (see recipe)
4 stalks celery, finely diced
½ red pepper, seeded and diced
¼ cup (60 mL) pine nuts or walnuts

Place apple in a salad bowl. To prevent browning sprinkle with lemon juice and let stand for 1 minute. Add all remaining ingredients. Serve chilled with your favorite salad dressing (see recipes).

Serves 6

FRENCH VEGETABLE SALAD

3 carrots, peeled and diced
½ lb (225 g) green beans, sliced
½ lb (225 g) green peas
½ small cauliflower, in florets
1 cucumber, diced
pepper to taste
Basic New Potato Salad (see recipe)

Boil or steam carrots and cauliflower together until just tender, about 10 minutes (or microwave, covered, with 1 tsp (5 mL) water on HIGH 5 minutes). Halfway through cooking, add peas and beans. Drain; reserve liquid and store for stock for soup recipes.

Combine vegetables with pepper and basic potato salad in a bowl and chill thoroughly. Serve with your favorite salad dressing (see recipes).

Serves 6

SEAFOOD SALAD

1 squid sac
milk, to soak
1 lb (450 g) uncooked shrimp
1 cup (250 mL) water
1 cup (250 mL) white wine
Basic New Potato Salad (see recipe)

Cut squid into thin strips. Place in a bowl, cover with milk and soak for at least 30 minutes. Peel shrimp, devein and cut in half lengthwise.

Combine water and wine in a pan and bring to a boil. Add shrimp and cook until just pink, then remove with a slotted spoon. Transfer to a salad bowl. Add squid to liquid, bring to a boil then drain on paper towels. Add to salad bowl; add potato salad and chill. Serve with French Dressing or Tasty Mayonnaise (see recipes).

Serves 6

CREAMY SALAD DRESSING

½ cup (125 mL) mayonnaise, store-bought or homemade (see Tasty Mayonnaise recipe)
¼ cup (60 mL) sour cream
¼ cup (60 mL) apple juice
3 egg yolks
3 tbsp (45 mL) virgin olive oil
1 tbsp (15 mL) lemon juice

Combine all ingredients in a blender and process until smooth. If mixing by hand, combine all ingredients except oil, beat well and very gradually add oil, beating until blended.

Makes approximately 1¼ cups (310 mL).

TASTY VARIATION:
☐ Replace oil and lemon juice with ¼ cup (60 mL) store-bought Italian dressing;
☐ replace apple juice with 1 peeled, sliced apple.

DILL DRESSING

3 tbsp (45 mL) white vinegar
2 tsp (10 mL) chopped fresh dill
½ cup (125 mL) virgin olive oil

Combine all ingredients in a screw-top jar and shake well.

Makes approximately ¾ cup (180 mL).

SALADE DOLOISE

6 slices ham, diced
¼ lb (110 g) green beans, sliced and cooked
2 green onions, diced
2 tomatoes, cut into wedges
Basic Potato Salad (see recipe)
Creamy Salad Dressing (see recipe)

Combine all salad ingredients in a salad bowl. Pour dressing over and chill.

Serves 6

HUANCAINA PAPAS

This is a traditional potato salad from the country which first cultivated potatoes – Peru.

1 cup (250 g) cottage cheese
freshly squeezed lemon juice
Basic Potato Salad (see recipe)
lettuce leaves
1 tsp (5 mL) paprika

Combine cottage cheese and lemon juice. Mix well, then add to the potato salad and stir with a fork. Serve on lettuce leaves and sprinkle with paprika.

Serves 6

HERRING POTATO SALAD

lettuce leaves, washed
7 oz (200 g) canned herrings in tomato sauce
Basic Potato Salad (see recipe)
1 dill pickle, sliced
Creamy Salad Dressing (see recipe)

Line a salad bowl with lettuce leaves. Break herrings into chunks and place in salad bowl with potato salad and pickle slices. Add tomato sauce from herrings to creamy salad dressing and pour over salad. Chill thoroughly and serve.

Serves 6

TASTY VARIATION:
☐ Replace herrings with 9 oz (250 g) sardines.

POTATO AND BEET SALAD WITH DILL DRESSING

8 oz (225 g) canned beets, whole or sliced
3 tbsp (45 mL) chopped fresh chives
Basic Potato Salad (see recipe)
Dill Dressing (see recipe)

Drain beets and combine with chives and potato salad in a salad bowl. Serve with dill dressing.

Serves 6

THE NUTRITIOUS POTATO				
3 oz (90 g) SERVING	BAKED	BOILED	MASHED	FRENCH FRIED
Protein	2.1 g	1.5 g	1.7 g	3.6 g
Fat	0.1 g	0.1 g	3.8 g	15 g
Carbohydrate	23 g	18 g	15 g	36 g
Calcium	9.0 mg	7.2 mg	23.4 mg	17.1 mg
Iron	1.2 mg	0.3 mg	0.2 mg	0.7 mg
Sodium	7.2 mg	4.5 mg	265 mg	200.0 mg
Vitamin A	0	0	18	0
Thiamine	0.1 mg	0.1 mg	.07 mg	0.16 mg
Riboflavin	.03 mg	0.02 mg	0.04 mg	0.03 mg
Niacin	1.4 mg	1.2 mg	1.0 mg	3 mg
Ascorbic acid	11.0 mg	6.3 mg	5.4 mg	9.0 mg
Calories	98	77	95	284

KEY
Gram – g
Milligram – mg

DRIED VERSUS FRESH
Dried herbs may be used instead of fresh herbs. Replace with a quarter of the recommended quantity of fresh herbs.
1 tbsp (15 mL) chopped fresh herbs = slightly less than 1 tsp (5 mL) dried

Delicious Dressings for Potato Salads

Dressings are crucial to any salad. For those who prefer a basic dressing, prepare your salad, take it to the table, and just before eating, pour on vinegar and oil, in the ratio of one part vinegar to two parts oil. For those who prefer something a little fancier, the range is endless. Try the following recipes, and experiment by creating your own.

CLASSIC DRESSING

1 tbsp (15 mL) cold water
yolks from 3 hard-boiled eggs
⅔ cup (165 mL) cream
1 tbsp (15 mL) white vinegar
¼ tsp (1 mL) cayenne pepper

Combine water and egg yolks in a blender. Add cream, vinegar and pepper and blend again. Chill. This mixture will thicken but should pour easily.

If mixing by hand, mix egg yolks to a paste with water, then add other ingredients very slowly.

Makes approximately ¾ cup (180 mL).

Classic Dressing, Herb Dressing and Tomato Dressing

HERB DRESSING

4 green onions, finely diced
1 clove garlic, crushed
1 tbsp (15 mL) chopped fresh parsley
3 tbsp (45 mL) chopped fresh basil
1 tbsp (15 mL) chopped fresh marjoram
1 tbsp (15 mL) chopped fresh thyme
½ cup (125 mL) virgin olive oil
3 tbsp (45 mL) white vinegar
½ tsp (2.5 mL) sugar
1 tbsp (15 mL) freshly squeezed lemon juice

Combine all ingredients and blend well.

Makes approximately 1 cup (250 mL).

TOMATO DRESSING

¼ cup (60 mL) catsup
¼ cup (60 mL) plain yogurt
3 tbsp (45 mL) virgin olive oil
1 tbsp (15 mL) freshly squeezed lemon juice

Combine all ingredients and mix well.

Makes approximately 3/4 cup (175 mL).

Main courses

Potato dishes can make filling, substantial meals.
Crêpes, soups, pies, soufflés, stews, quiches, rolls, pastries,
potatoes with fish, chicken, meat and vegetables
– this selection can feed the family and provide the basis
for many successful dinner parties.

LUSCIOUS POTATO CRÊPES

1 cup (250 g) cream cheese
1 tbsp (15 mL) flour
2 eggs, beaten
1 cup (125 g) grated strong Cheddar
  cheese
4 potatoes, peeled and grated
  (squeeze out excess moisture)
pepper to taste
1 tbsp (15 mL) chopped fresh parsley
¼ – ½ cup (60-125 mL) cream or milk
1 tbsp (15 mL) oil or butter

FILLINGS
1. 6 mushrooms, sautéed;
2. ¼ cup (60 mL) ham, diced, or
   chicken, cooked and diced,
   1 tbsp (15 mL) chopped chives
   and ¼ cup (60 mL) sour cream;
3. ¼ lb (110 g) chicken livers cooked
   and 1 onion, sliced and sautéed;
4. 2 slices bacon and 1 tomato,
   chopped and fried together;
5. 1 green apple, cored and diced,
   mixed with ¼ cup (60 mL) blue
   cheese and 1½ tbsp (20 mL)
   chopped walnuts;
6. 1 cup (250 mL) cooked chopped
   spinach, 1½ tbsp (20 mL) pine nuts
   and 1 clove garlic, crushed, all
   fried in 1½ tbsp (20 mL) butter.

Mash cream cheese and flour together.
Beat in eggs, cheese, grated potatoes,
pepper and parsley. Add sufficient cream
to make a thick batter.

Heat oil in small frying pan. Pour in
1 tbsp (15 mL) batter; move pan to
spread batter over base. Brown both
sides. To keep crêpes warm, stack on a
plate, cover with foil and set over a pan of
simmering water.

Serve crêpes with the filling of your
choice in the center, or serve with bacon,
a salad or as an accompaniment to other
dishes.

Serves 6

POTATO OMELET

4 medium potatoes, peeled and
  cooked
6 eggs, separated
2 onions, grated
1 tsp (5 mL) chopped fresh parsley
pepper to taste
3 tbsp (45 mL) butter

FILLINGS
3 tbsp (45 mL) grated Cheddar cheese
  per omelet or
2 slices bacon, diced and cooked
  until crisp or
4 mushrooms, sliced and sautéed
  with 3 tbsp (45 mL) grated cheese

Preheat oven to 275°F (140°C).

Drain and mash potatoes with egg
yolks, onions, parsley and pepper. Whisk
egg whites until stiff and fold into potato
mixture.

Melt butter in a frying pan, swirling to
coat the pan. Pour in one-sixth of the
potato mixture. Gently move mixture
around until just starting to set. Cook until
the omelet sets, then carefully ease onto
a plate using a spatula.

Place a spoonful of filling on one side of
the omelet and fold over. Place in oven to
keep warm. Repeat until all six omelets
have been made. Serve with bacon or
salad.

Serves 6

INSTANT GRAVY THICKENER
If your gravy needs thickening, add
1 tbsp (15 mL) or so of mashed
potato.

Luscious Potato Crêpes

FISHERMAN'S PIE

1½ lbs (700 g) white fish fillets
  (see Note)
pepper to taste
1 cup (250 mL) milk
1 tbsp (15 mL) lemon juice
1½ tbsp (20 mL) butter

SAUCE
¼ cup (60 mL) butter
3 tbsp (45 mL) flour
1 cup (250 mL) milk
2 hard-boiled eggs, shelled and sliced
¼ cup (60 mL) chopped fresh
  parsley
1 tbsp (15 mL) capers, drained
¼ lb (110 g) shrimp, peeled and cooked

TOPPING
4 medium potatoes, cooked and
  mashed
1½ tbsp (20 mL) butter
½ cup (125 mL) sour cream
pinch nutmeg

Arrange fish fillets in an ovenproof dish and season with pepper. Pour milk and lemon juice over fillets and dot with butter. Cover and bake at 350°F (180°C) for 15–20 minutes (or microwave on HIGH 8 minutes, using ½ cup (125 mL) of milk only).

Reserve any cooking liquid. Remove any skin and flake fish into large pieces.

To make the sauce, melt butter in a pan and stir in flour. Cook for 1 minute. Remove from heat. Gradually stir in milk and reserved cooking liquid. Return to heat and bring to a boil, stirring well until mixture thickens.

(To microwave sauce, place butter in a cup, microwave on HIGH 1 minute. Add flour and microwave on HIGH 1 minute, gradually stirring in milk and reserved cooking liquid. Microwave on HIGH 3–4 minutes until the mixture boils and thickens.)

Add sliced hard-boiled eggs to the sauce; then add the fish, parsley, capers and shrimp. Spoon back into the ovenproof dish.

To make topping, combine mashed potatoes with butter and sour cream. Spoon onto fish mixture and sprinkle with nutmeg. Return to oven and heat for approximately 15 minutes (or microwave on HIGH 3 minutes). Serve with salad or cooked vegetables.

Serves 6

Note: Sole, halibut, haddock or bluefish fillets are delicious white fish to use. Also ideal for this recipe is smoked cod or haddock. Cooking the smoked fish in the milk takes away the strong salty flavor.

TASTY VARIATION:
☐ To make a more colorful dish, leave out the shrimp, and substitute 2 tomatoes, chopped, or ½ cup (50 g) cooked peas or sliced carrots.

1. *Pour milk over fish fillets in an ovenproof dish.*

2. *Flake fish into large pieces.*

3. To make sauce, melt butter and stir in flour.

4. To make topping, combine mashed potatoes, butter and sour cream.

5. Spoon topping over fish mixture and return to oven.

Meaty Potato Courses

On the following two pages, you will find some well-known recipes which feature both meat and potatoes. These hearty dishes are particularly suitable for cold winter nights, dinner parties or extra-hungry teenagers.

CORNISH PASTIES

½ lb (225 g) round steak, trimmed and diced
2 medium potatoes, peeled and diced
3 tbsp (45 mL) chopped fresh parsley
2 carrots, peeled and diced
2 onions, diced
3 tbsp (45 mL) fresh peas
¼ cup (60 mL) water
1 cube beef stock
3 tbsp (45 mL) catsup
3 tbsp (45 mL) flour
double quantity Pastry Crust (see recipe)
1 egg yolk
1 tbsp (15 mL) milk

In a pan, combine meat, potatoes, parsley, carrots, onions, peas, water and stock cube and bring to a boil. Simmer 10 minutes then remove from heat and cool thoroughly. Drain, reserving liquid to mix with catsup and flour to make gravy.

Preheat oven to 475°F (250°C). Cut pastry into three portions. Roll out one portion into a square and cut in half. Mix egg yolk and milk together and brush over all pastry edges to glaze. Place one-sixth of vegetable mixture in center of each half, and fold to form a triangle. Press edges together with fingers, making a frilled edge. Place on a greased baking tray.

Repeat with remaining pastry and filling. Brush all triangles with remaining egg-milk mixture and bake approximately 30 minutes until crisp and brown. While baking, make gravy. Combine reserved liquid, catsup and flour and bring to a boil, stirring until gravy thickens (or microwave on HIGH 3 minutes or until gravy boils and thickens). Serve hot with pasties.

Makes 6

Note: Uncooked, prepared pasties can be frozen for up to three months. Allow an extra 5 minutes cooking time.

PASTRY CRUST

1 cup (125 mL) flour
pinch salt
¼ cup (60 mL) butter
1 egg yolk
1 tbsp (15 mL) lemon juice
cold water
1 egg beaten with 3 tbsp (45 mL) milk, to glaze

Place flour and salt in a bowl. Add butter. With fingertips only, mix to a bread crumb consistency. Mix in egg yolk and lemon juice. With a knife, cut in 1 tbsp (15 mL) water, adding a little more if necessary to form a stiff dough.

Turn out onto a floured board and knead gently into a smooth ball. If using to make a pie, roll out to size of pie plate. Carefully line pie plate with crust. Prick base with a fork. Bake at 350°F (180°C) for 15–20 minutes or until golden brown.

Makes bottom crust for one 8-inch (20 cm) pie.

STORING PIE CRUSTS
The cooked crust will keep for 5 days in an airtight container. When making it, make double the quantity. Freeze half. Pastry, either cooked or uncooked, can be frozen for up to 3 months.

1. Cut pastry into three portions.

2. Roll out each portion and cut in half.

3. Spoon one-sixth of filling onto each.

LAMB NAVARIN WITH NEW POTATOES

1 lb (450 g) lamb stewing chops
1½ tbsp (20 mL) butter
2 onions, diced
1 clove garlic, crushed
3 carrots, peeled and diced
¼ cup (60 mL) flour
1 tbsp (15 mL) tomato paste
pinch dried thyme
1 bay leaf
pepper to taste
2 cups (500 mL) canned beef consommé
½ cup (125 mL) water
6 new potatoes, washed
3 tbsp (45 mL) chopped fresh parsley

Arrange chops in an ovenproof casserole dish.

Melt butter in a pan, add onions and fry until transparent, then add garlic and carrots. Add flour, tomato paste, thyme, bay leaf, pepper, beef consommé and water. Stir until smooth. Bring to a boil then pour over chops. Add potatoes and parsley. Bake, covered, at 350°F (180°C) for 1½ hours.

Serves 6

BEEF BOURGUIGNON

2 lbs (1 kg) boneless lean beef
flour, for coating
1½ tbsp (20 mL) butter
1 clove garlic, crushed
2 slices bacon, diced
1 cube beef stock
6–8 small new potatoes, washed
6–8 small onions, peeled
pinch dried thyme
1 bay leaf
½ cup (125 mL) water
½ cup (125 mL) red wine
¼ cup (60 mL) brandy

Trim fat off meat. Cut meat into cubes and toss in flour to coat. Melt butter, add garlic and bacon and lightly fry. Add meat and brown.

Transfer to a casserole dish. Crumble stock cube over meat and add all remaining ingredients.

Cover and cook in the oven at 350°F (180°C) for 1½ hours.

Serve hot with green vegetables or a green salad.

Serves 6

TASTY VARIATION:
☐ Add ¼ lb (110 g) small mushrooms 20 minutes before the dish has finished cooking.

POTATOES WITH BEEF 'N' BEER

1 lb (450 g) boneless lean beef
1 oz (28 g) package French onion soup mix
2 potatoes, peeled and diced
1½ cups (375 mL) beer
1 loaf French bread
Dijon mustard
grated strong Cheddar cheese

Trim fat off beef. Cut beef into cubes and toss in the onion soup mixture to coat. In a pan, combine beef, potatoes and beer and bring to a boil. Simmer 1½ hours.

When cooked, spoon into six individual bowls. Cut bread into six thick slices, spread with Dijon mustard and place a slice on top of meat in each bowl, mustard side down.

Top with grated cheese and brown under broiler (or microwave on HIGH until the cheese melts and bubbles). Serve as a complete dish or accompanied by green vegetables or salad.

Serves 6

TASTY VARIATION:
☐ 1 cup (100 g) sliced vegetables, e.g. peas or carrots, can be added and cooked with the meat.

POTATO QUICHE

3 tbsp (45 mL) butter
1 onion, sliced
1 clove garlic, crushed
2 medium potatoes, peeled and grated
3 eggs
3 tbsp (45 mL) diced ham
3 tbsp (45 mL) grated strong Cheddar cheese
1 tbsp (15 mL) chopped fresh parsley
1 tbsp (15 mL) chopped fresh chives
6½ oz (185 g) prepared pastry or 1 Pastry Crust (see recipe)

Melt butter, add onion and garlic and fry until transparent (or microwave on HIGH 2 minutes). Add grated potatoes. Whisk eggs and add with ham, cheese, parsley and chives to potato-onion mixture. Pour into prepared crust and bake in the oven at 350°F (180°C) for 1 hour. Serve with salad.

Serves 6

TASTY VARIATION:
☐ Replace ham with 3 tbsp (45 g) chopped mushrooms, add to onion and sauté.

CURRIED MEATBALLS

2 slices bread
½ cup (125 mL) milk
1¾ lbs (800 g) ground beef
2 eggs, beaten
1 onion, diced
pepper to taste
1 tbsp (15 mL) curry powder
4 potatoes, peeled and diced
2 carrots, peeled and diced
1¼ cups (310 mL) tomato purée or sauce
pinch cayenne pepper
pinch ground cumin
pinch ground coriander

Cut crusts from bread and discard (see *Note*). Place bread in a bowl, cover with milk and soak for 5 minutes. Combine ground beef, eggs, onion, pepper and half the curry powder. Squeeze the milk from the bread and add bread to ground beef mixture. Roll mixture into small balls and chill.

Cook potatoes and carrots in a pan with a little water for 10 minutes (or microwave, covered, with 2 tsp (10 mL) water on HIGH 5 minutes). Stir in tomato paste, remaining curry powder, cayenne pepper, cumin, coriander and meatballs and simmer for 30 minutes (or microwave on HIGH 5 minutes, on MEDIUM 8 minutes. Let stand for 4 minutes). Serve with steamed rice.

Serves 6

Note: Cut crusts into cubes and bake in a 350°F (180°C) oven until crisp and brown. Use as croutons for soup.

TASTY VARIATIONS:
☐ Replace beef with ground pork or veal;
☐ Replace cayenne, cumin and coriander with 1 tbsp (15 mL) of garam masala.

WATERY BOILED POTATOES
If your boiled potatoes taste too watery, add a little powdered milk.

FULLER FLAVOR
Cook a casserole 24 hours before serving, as it develops a much richer flavor.

Split Pea and Potato Soup, and Minestrone

CAULIFLOWER SOUP

1 small cauliflower, broken into florets
1 onion, sliced
3 medium potatoes, peeled and sliced
1 chicken stock cube
2 cups (500 mL) water
grated strong Cheddar cheese, to sprinkle

In a pan, combine cauliflower florets, onion, potatoes, stock cube and water. Bring to a boil and simmer until vegetables are very tender, about 30 minutes. Blend until smooth or mash well and push through a sieve.

To serve, reheat and spoon into soup bowls (or microwave on HIGH 2 minutes per bowl). Sprinkle with cheese.

Serves 4–6 (depending on size of cauliflower)

CORN AND POTATO SOUP

1½ tbsp (20 mL) butter
2 onions, sliced
4 medium potatoes, peeled and sliced
3 cups (750 mL) water
2 chicken stock cubes
½ cup (125 mL) cream
16 oz (440 g) canned creamed corn
1 tbsp (15 mL) chopped fresh chives, to serve

Melt butter in a pan, add onion and gently fry until transparent. Add potatoes, water and stock cubes and bring to a boil. Lower heat and simmer for 30 minutes. Blend or push through a sieve until smooth. Return to the pan and add cream and corn. Reheat but do not boil. (Alternatively, add cream and corn and microwave on MEDIUM for 4 minutes.)

Serve in soup bowls sprinkled with chives.

Serves 6

TASTY VARIATIONS:
☐ Replace chives with 2 tsp (10 mL) nutmeg, or 3 tbsp (45 mL) grated strong Cheddar cheese;
☐ add 3 stalks celery, diced, to the blended soup before serving.

MINESTRONE

4 slices bacon, diced
1 onion, diced
1 cup (250 mL) chopped fresh parsley
1 clove garlic, crushed
1 stalk celery, diced
2 medium potatoes, peeled and diced
2 carrots, peeled and diced
1 zucchini, diced
¼ lb (110 g) green beans, stringed and chopped
11 oz (310 g) canned red kidney beans, drained
3 tomatoes, peeled and chopped
6 cups (1.5 L) water
1 cup (250 mL) uncooked white rice, optional
¼ lb (110 g) cabbage, shredded
grated Parmesan cheese, to serve
crusty bread, to serve

Combine diced bacon and onion in a pan and fry for 1 minute. Add all the vegetables except cabbage and cover with water. Bring to a boil and simmer for 1 hour. If using white rice, add and cook 30 minutes more. Add cabbage and simmer another 30 minutes. Pour into a tureen and serve with a bowl of Parmesan cheese and crusty bread.

Serves 6

SPLIT PEA AND POTATO SOUP

1 lb (450 g) dried peas
6 cups (1.5 L) water
1 lb (450 g) ham bones
3 large potatoes, peeled and sliced
2 onions, sliced
2 stalks celery, diced
1 cup (250 mL) milk
croutons or bacon bits, to serve

Soak dried peas overnight in 3 cups (750 mL) water.

Next day strain and discard the water. Place 3 cups (750 mL) water in a pan with ham bones and simmer for 1 hour. Add peas, potatoes, onions and celery and simmer for another hour. Remove bones and scrape off meat. Discard bones and return meat to the soup.

Blend till smooth or mash well and push through a sieve. Add sufficient milk to reach the thickness you prefer. Reheat (or microwave on HIGH 5 minutes).

Serve with croutons or bacon.

Serves 6

TASTY VARIATION:
☐ Add 1 carrot, diced, to the vegetables when cooking.

POTATOES AND SWISS CHARD WITH FETTUCCINE

½ lb (225 g) red potatoes, peeled and cut into ½ inch (1 cm) diced pieces
1 small bunch Swiss chard, rinsed, leaves and stalks separated
⅓ cup (85 mL) butter
3 cloves garlic, crushed
1 Spanish onion, coarsely chopped
1 tbsp (15 mL) finely chopped fresh sage, oregano or parsley
½ red pepper, julienned
1 lb (450 g) fresh fettuccine or ¾ lb (340 g) dried
1 cup (250 mL) grated Mozzarella cheese
⅓ cup (85 mL) grated Parmesan cheese
salt and pepper, to taste

In a saucepan of boiling salted water, boil potatoes until tender-crisp for 3–4 minutes; remove with a slotted spoon and set aside.

Slice Swiss chard stalks into ½ inch (1 cm) pieces. Slice leaves into thin strips and place in a large colander.

In the saucepan of boiling water cook Swiss chard stalks for 5–6 minutes. Now pour the contents of the saucepan, including the water, over the leaves in the colander. Turn over with a wooden spoon and leave to drain and cool in the sink.

Melt butter in a large frying pan and gently sauté garlic, onion and herbs for 5–6 minutes. Do not brown the onion, only soften it. Add potatoes, chard stalks and leaves and red pepper and toss lightly. Cover and cook for 5 minutes.

Cook and drain fettuccine and transfer to a large buttered shallow ovenproof dish. Add the Swiss chard mixture and toss to combine. Add cheeses, season and toss again.

Cover and bake at 375°F (190°C) for 20 minutes, or until cheeses are melted through and bubbling.

Serves 4

BAKED TORTELLINI

½ lb (225 g) eggplant
salt
½ lb (225 g) tortellini, filled with beef or cheese
½ lb (225 g) potatoes, peeled and cut into 3/4 inch (2 cm) slices
½ cup (125 mL) olive oil
1 onion, sliced thinly
1¾ cups (440 mL) canned peeled plum tomatoes
½ tsp (2.5 mL) chopped fresh oregano
pinch cayenne pepper
salt and pepper to taste
1 cup (250 mL) shredded Mozzarella cheese
3 tbsp (45 mL) extra chopped fresh oregano or parsley

Dice eggplant into ¾ inch (2 cm) pieces, sprinkle with salt and leave to drain over the sink in a colander or strainer.

Boil tortellini and when cooked drain and place in a shallow ovenproof dish.

In a small saucepan, boil potatoes until just cooked; drain. Heat some oil in a frying pan and sauté potatoes until brown, then add to the tortellini.

With a little more oil, sauté onion gently for 5 minutes and then add drained eggplant. Continue cooking, adding more oil if necessary, until the eggplant is tender and golden.

Drain tomatoes and add to the pan, breaking them up with a wooden spoon while stirring in. Add seasonings and cook for 5–8 minutes, or until the tomatoes have reduced and there is little liquid left.

Add to the dish with tortellini and stir in one-third of the Mozzarella. Distribute remaining Mozzarella over the top and sprinkle with extra oregano or parsley.

Bake at 375°F (190°C) for 10 minutes so cheese melts and bubbles on top.

Serves 4

Baked Tortellini, Potatoes and Swiss Chard with Fettuccine

SALMON ROLLS

6 whole cabbage leaves (or outer leaves of lettuce)
2 carrots, grated
1 lb (450 g) canned red salmon, drained
4 medium potatoes, cooked and mashed
3 tbsp (45 mL) mayonnaise
2 cups (500 mL) water
3 tbsp (45 mL) tomato paste
1 chicken stock cube
1½ tbsp (20 mL) cornstarch mixed with 2½ tbsp (40 mL) water
crusty bread, to serve

Remove any thick stalks from the cabbage. Place leaves in a pan carefully to avoid breaking them. Cover with water and bring to a boil. Remove from heat and let stand 3 minutes (or microwave on HIGH 2 minutes; allow to cool before removing from microwave). Drain and pat dry.

Combine grated carrots with salmon, potatoes and mayonnaise. Spoon equal quantities into the center of each cabbage leaf and roll carefully, tucking the ends under. Arrange in an ovenproof dish in a single layer.

Combine water, tomato paste and crumbled stock cube and pour over salmon rolls. Bake uncovered in the oven at 350°F (180°C) for 45 minutes (or microwave on HIGH 15 minutes using only 1 cup (250 mL) water mixed with tomato paste and stock cube).

Remove rolls, set aside and keep warm. Pour stock into a pan and mix in cornstarch paste. Stir over heat until the mixture boils and thickens (or microwave on HIGH 2 minutes).

Cut salmon rolls in half. Place two halves on each plate and spoon on some of the thickened stock. Serve with crusty warm bread.

Serves 6

TASTY VARIATION:
☐ Replace salmon with ½ lb (225 g) cooked, diced chicken.

SHORTCUTS
5 tbsp (75 mL) of instant potato mixed with hot water is a quick replacement for 2 medium potatoes, cooked.

FISH PARCELS

1½ tbsp (20 mL) butter
1 onion, sliced
2 potatoes, peeled and thinly sliced
2 tomatoes, sliced
1 green pepper, seeded and sliced
6 fresh fish fillets
oil
3 tbsp (45 mL) lemon juice
¼ cup (60 mL) white wine
1 tbsp (15 mL) chopped fresh chives
1½ tbsp (20 mL) cornstarch mixed with 2½ tbsp (40 mL) water

Melt butter, add onion and fry until transparent (or microwave together on HIGH 2 minutes). Add potatoes, tomatoes and green pepper and stir for 1 minute (or microwave on HIGH 45 seconds).

Lightly oil six pieces of aluminum foil (or microwave-proof plastic wrap). Place a piece of fish on each piece of foil and spoon mixed vegetables on top. Sprinkle with lemon juice, wine and chives. Fold foil around fish mixture to make a parcel.

Arrange in a baking dish and bake at 350°F (180°C) for 30 minutes (or microwave on HIGH 8–10 minutes, checking to see when fish is cooked). Carefully make a small hole in the foil and pour off liquid into a pan. Stir cornstarch paste into fish liquid and heat until sauce thickens (or combine fish juices and cornstarch paste and microwave on HIGH 2 minutes.)

To serve, carefully unwrap fish, slide onto plates and cover with sauce.

Serves 6

TASTY VARIATION:
☐ Replace fish with 6 pork or lamb chops, trimmed of fat, and cook with vegetables in 350°F (180°C) oven 45 minutes.

MEAT LOAF WITH TASTY TOMATO TOPPING

2 medium potatoes, cooked and dry mashed
1 lb (450 g) ground beef
1 egg
1 oz (28 g) package French onion soup mix
1 cup (250 mL) milk

TOPPING
¼ cup (60 mL) catsup
pinch dry mustard
1 tbsp (15 mL) brown sugar

Combine potatoes, beef, egg, French onion soup mix and milk. Mix well and spoon into a meat loaf pan.

Combine topping ingredients and spread over the top of the meat loaf. Bake at 350°F (180°C) for 1 hour (or microwave on HIGH 25 minutes. Let stand for 5 minutes before serving).

Serve hot with vegetables, or cold with a salad. This recipe is also great to freeze and serve in an emergency.

Serves 6

TASTY VARIATIONS:
☐ 1 lb (450 g) mixture of ground lamb and pork; or
☐ three pineapple slices placed on top before baking.

SEMOLINA GNOCCHI WITH VEAL AND TOMATO SAUCE

GNOCCHI
3 medium potatoes, cooked and dry mashed
1½ cups (375 mL) milk
¾ cup (100 g) fine semolina
1 tsp (5 mL) nutmeg
2 eggs, beaten

VEAL AND TOMATO SAUCE
3 tbsp (45 mL) butter
1 onion, sliced
2 cloves garlic, crushed
1 lb (450 g) ground veal
2¼ cups (560 mL) canned tomatoes, drained and liquid reserved
3 tbsp (45 mL) tomato paste
2 cups (500 mL) white wine
1 cup (250 mL) water
2 chicken stock cubes
1 tsp (5 mL) sugar
1 tsp (5 mL) chopped fresh basil leaves
grated Parmesan cheese to garnish
3 tbsp (45 mL) chopped fresh parsley to garnish

In a pan, combine mashed potatoes and milk. Bring to a simmer. Add semolina and nutmeg and stir until mixture becomes thick and very stiff. Remove from heat and beat in eggs. Spoon into a greased casserole dish and leave overnight. When ready, cut into squares and cook in boiling water. Boil for 1 minute after gnocchi rise to the top of pan, then remove with a slotted spoon. Drain on paper towels and set aside to keep warm.

To make sauce, melt butter in a pan, add onion and fry until transparent (or microwave butter and onion on HIGH 2 minutes). Stir in remaining ingredients (including liquid from tomatoes) and bring to a boil. Simmer 1½ hours uncovered.

Pour sauce over gnocchi and garnish with a sprinkle of Parmesan cheese and fresh parsley.

Serves 4–6

FISH À LA GRECQUE

2 potatoes, peeled and sliced
2 onions, sliced
½ lb (225 g) fresh fish fillets
2 tomatoes, sliced
1 tbsp (15 mL) safflower oil
½ cup (125 mL) water
pepper to taste
3 tbsp (45 mL) chopped fresh parsley

Grease a casserole dish. Arrange potatoes and onions in the bottom, with fish fillets on top. Cover with sliced tomatoes.

Mix together oil, water, pepper and parsley and pour over casserole. Bake at 350°F (180°C) for 30 minutes (or microwave on HIGH 8 minutes). Serve with a salad and fresh bread.

Serves 6

TASTY VARIATION:
☐ Replace fresh tomatoes with 2 cups (500 mL) canned tomatoes, sliced, and use tomato liquid in place of water.

SAUTÉED POTATOES WITH CHICKEN AND MUSHROOMS

Although this dish is made with chicken it is delicious with any leftover cooked meat.

3 medium potatoes, peeled, sliced
  and cooked
1 tbsp (15 mL) oil
pepper to taste
1½ tbsp (20 mL) butter
1 onion, peeled and sliced
¼ lb (110 g) mushrooms, sliced
½ lb (225 g) cooked chicken meat
½ cup (125 mL) cream
1 tbsp (15 mL) sherry
pinch paprika

Drain the potatoes and carefully pat dry with paper towels.

In a frying pan heat oil and fry potatoes until golden brown. Season and remove with a slotted spoon. Keep hot in the oven at 350°F (180°C), (or microwave on HIGH 2 minutes when ready to use).

In the same pan, melt butter and fry onion until transparent. Stir in mushrooms and cook a further 1 minute. Add chicken meat and cook, stirring, for 4 minutes (or microwave butter and onion on HIGH 2 minutes, add mushrooms and chicken meat and cook on HIGH 2 minutes).

Add cream and sherry, bring to a boil and simmer 5 minutes (or microwave cream and sherry on MEDIUM 2 minutes). To serve, spoon vegetable-chicken mixture into a large warmed serving dish and surround with potatoes. Sprinkle with paprika.

Serves 6

Fish à la Grecque, Sautéed Potatoes with Chicken and Mushrooms, and Semolina Gnocchi with Veal and Tomato Sauce

POTATO SOUFFLÉ WITH TANGY BACON SAUCE

3 medium potatoes, peeled and cooked
1½ tbsp (20 mL) butter
⅓ cup (85 mL) sour cream
1 tbsp (15 mL) chopped fresh chives
pepper to taste
4 eggs, separated
1 cup (250 mL) grated strong Cheddar cheese

TANGY BACON SAUCE
1½ tbsp (20 mL) butter
4 slices bacon, diced
¼ cup (60 mL) catsup
1 tbsp (15 mL) Worcestershire sauce
3 tbsp (45 mL) water
2 chicken stock cubes

Mash potatoes until smooth with butter, sour cream, chives, pepper, yolks and cheese. Whisk egg whites until stiff. Carefully fold into potato mixture. Spoon into a greased soufflé dish, running a knife in a circle 1 inch (2.5 cm) deep into the center of the mixture. (This will, when cooked, form a raised top). Stand in a dish of warm water and bake at 350°F (180°C) for 45 minutes, or until a knife inserted in the side of the soufflé comes out clean. Serve immediately with sauce.

To make sauce, melt butter, add bacon and gently fry until crisp (or microwave butter and bacon, covered, on HIGH, 4 minutes).

Stir in remaining ingredients and bring to a boil, stirring (or microwave other ingredients on HIGH 2 minutes). Serve hot.

Serves 6

TASTY VARIATIONS:
Add to the potato mixture any of the following:
☐ 3 tbsp (45 g) corn and ½ green pepper finely diced;
☐ 3 tbsp (45 g) bacon, diced and cooked, and 1 onion, diced and fried.

POTATO PANCAKES WITH SOUR CREAM AND APPLESAUCE

3 large potatoes, peeled and grated
6 green onions, finely chopped
2 eggs, beaten
⅓ cup (85 mL) dried bread crumbs
butter and oil
sour cream, to serve

APPLESAUCE
1 lb (450 g) cooking apples, peeled, cored and sliced

¼ cup (60 mL) sugar
Squeeze moisture from grated potatoes. Combine in a bowl with green onions, eggs and bread crumbs.

In a heavy-based frying pan, melt equal quantities of butter and oil, about 1 tbsp (15 mL) of each at a time. Drop in spoonfuls of potato mixture, fry and flip over. Cook until golden on both sides.

To make applesauce, cook sliced apples in a saucepan with enough water to avoid burning them, until apples form a soft pulp. Add sugar, stir to dissolve and serve with pancakes and sour cream.

Serves 4

OMELET WITH CRISPY PAN-FRIED POTATOES

Ideally use two pans, one for the omelet and the other for the filling. If using only one pan cook the filling first, set aside to keep warm, then cook the omelet.

4 medium potatoes, peeled and diced
¼ cup (60 mL) oil
4 slices bacon, diced
1 onion, peeled and diced
8 button mushrooms, washed and sliced

OMELET
12 eggs (allow 2 per person)
pepper to taste
½ cup (125 mL) butter

Boil potatoes until tender (or microwave potatoes, covered, with 1 tsp (5 mL) water, on HIGH 8 minutes). Heat oil, add bacon and onion and gently fry until onion is transparent. Add mushrooms and stir 2 minutes. Remove all ingredients with a slotted spoon and drain on paper towels.

Place cooked potatoes in pan and stir until brown. If potatoes start to stick add a little more oil. Return other ingredients to pan and stir until heated through. Divide potato mixture into sixths.

Preheat oven to 275°F (140°C).

To make omelet beat 2 eggs lightly and season with pepper. Melt 1½ tbsp (20 mL) butter in the pan. Add eggs as butter begins to froth – don't allow the butter to brown. Swirl eggs around the pan, forking them into the center so the remaining liquid can run into the spaces and cook. Continue cooking until the eggs have set underneath but are still moist on top. Carefully ease omelet onto a warmed plate. Spoon one-sixth of potato mixture onto omelet and fold over. Place in oven to keep warm. Repeat until all six omelets have been made.

Serves 6

FINNISH PIE

2 oz (60 g) dried mushrooms (see Glossary)
3 tbsp (45 mL) butter
1 onion, sliced
1 slice bacon, diced
2 lbs (1 kg) fresh mushrooms, wiped and sliced
pepper to taste
3 tbsp (45 mL) cream
½ cup (125 mL) dried bread crumbs

PUREE
4 medium potatoes, cooked
1 cup (250 mL) hot milk
1 egg, beaten
1½ tbsp (20 mL) butter

Soak dried mushrooms in hot water for 10 minutes; drain, squeeze dry and chop finely. Melt butter in a pan and fry onion and bacon until bacon is crisp (or microwave butter, onion and bacon on HIGH 3 minutes). Add all the mushrooms and pepper and fry for 2 minutes (or microwave mushrooms and pepper on HIGH 2 minutes). Stir in cream.

Mash potatoes with hot milk, then beat in egg and butter to form a purée.

Grease a shallow dish and pour in half the potato purée, add the mushroom mixture and top with remaining purée. Sprinkle with bread crumbs and dot with butter. Bake in the oven at 350°F (180°C) for 20 minutes (or microwave on HIGH 4 minutes). Serve with pickles or a green salad.

Serves 6

TASTY VARIATION:
☐ Replace mushrooms and bacon with 12 fresh scallops. Cover the scallops with cream and allow to stand for 20 minutes. This makes the scallops juicy and plump. Use the cream in the sauce.

Potato Pancakes with Sour Cream and Applesauce

Classic Accompaniments

In many countries, potatoes are served with a main meal at least once a day. The French, in particular, have adopted the potato as their own, and to them we owe many of the superb dishes found in restaurants around the world. Some of our recipes make serving suggestions, but you can enjoy them with almost anything.

POTATOES ANNA

6 large potatoes, peeled, washed and thinly sliced
½ lb (225 g) butter

Thickly grease six small custard cups with butter. Arrange a layer of potatoes in a circle in the base of each custard cup and top with a small piece of butter. Repeat, reversing the circle. Allow 3 tbsp (45 mL) of butter per cup. Continue, reversing each time, until all the cups are filled.

Stand cups in ½ inch (1 cm) hot water in a baking dish. Cover cups with foil. Bake at 350°F (180°C) for 1 hour or until potatoes are tender. (Alternatively, cover with microwave-proof plastic wrap and microwave on HIGH 5 minutes, then MEDIUM 10 minutes or until tender.)

Gently tilt each cup to pour off excess butter. Place a dinner plate on top of the cup and turn upside down. Carefully lift cup from potatoes.

Serves 6

DUCHESSE POTATOES

6 large potatoes, cooked and sliced
2 egg yolks
⅓ cup (85 mL) butter
pinch nutmeg
1 egg, beaten

Mash potatoes with egg yolks, butter and nutmeg. Push mixture through a sieve into an icing bag fitted with a star nozzle. Pipe potatoes onto a greased oven tray, forming medium-sized stars.

Brush with beaten egg and bake in the oven at 350°F (180°C) until golden.

Serves 6

POTATOES ROMANOFF

6 medium potatoes, peeled
6 green onions, finely sliced
1¼ cups (310 mL) grated strong Cheddar cheese
1¼ cups (310 mL) sour cream
1 cup (250 mL) milk
pepper to taste
½ tsp (2.5 mL) nutmeg

Cut potatoes in half and cook in boiling water until firm but tender (or microwave whole potatoes on HIGH 8 minutes). Allow to cool.

Coarsely grate potatoes into a greased casserole dish. Add green onions and half the cheese. Combine cream, milk and pepper. Pour over potato and cheese, then top with remaining cheese and the nutmeg.

Chill for 2 hours or overnight. Bake uncovered in the oven at 350°F (180°C) for 40 minutes.

Serves 6

LYONNAISE POTATOES

6 tbsp (90 mL) butter
4 large potatoes, peeled and thinly sliced
2 onions, thinly sliced

Melt 3 tbsp (45 mL) butter in a pan, add potatoes, turning until tender and golden brown. While potatoes are cooking, in a separate pan, melt remaining butter and fry onions until tender. Combine to serve. Serve with broiled meats.

Serves 6

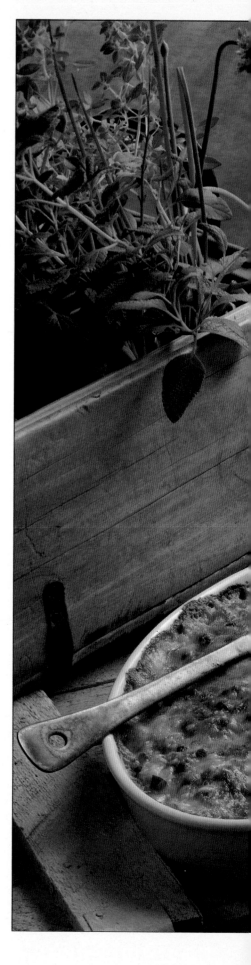

Potatoes Romanoff, Lyonnaise Potatoes

Cheesy Potato Fans served with a rack of lamb

SUGAR-GLAZED POTATOES

12 small new potatoes, washed
¼ cup (60 mL) white sugar
3 tbsp (45 mL) butter

Boil potatoes until tender (or prick and microwave on HIGH 8 minutes in a covered dish). Drain and chill thoroughly.

Dissolve sugar in a heavy pan, add butter and stir to combine. Add potatoes and stir until browned. Serve immediately.

Serves 6

Handy hints: Cook potatoes the day before and store in refrigerator to chill overnight.

DRY ROASTED POTATOES

6 potatoes, peeled and cut in half
lengthwise

Place potatoes on an oven rack and dry roast for 30 minutes in the oven at 400°F (200°C).

Serves 6

HONEYED ROAST POTATOES

2 medium potatoes, peeled
3 tbsp (45 mL) oil
¼ cup (60 mL) butter
salt (optional)
¼ cup (60 mL) honey

Add potatoes to a pan of cold water, bring to a boil then drain immediately.

Place potatoes in a baking dish with oil and butter and sprinkle with a little salt (see *Note*).

Bake at 350°F (180°C) for 20 minutes. Baste with honey and bake 20 minutes more. Serve with roasts.

Serves 2

Note: Sprinkling potatoes with a little salt gives a light, crunchy crust. But only small amounts of salt are necessary.

CHEESY POTATO FANS

6 large potatoes, peeled
oil
⅔ cup (165 mL) grated strong Cheddar
cheese
1 ½ tbsp (20 mL) butter

Cut a small slice from the end of each potato to make a flat base. Place potato, base down, on a large spoon and make a cut ¾ inch (2 cm) deep, or until the knife touches the edge of the spoon. Repeat with each potato.

Stand potatoes completely covered in cold water for 30 minutes, then drain and pat dry. Just cover the bottom of a baking dish with oil and brush each potato with oil. Stand potatoes in the dish and bake at 350°F (180°C) for 1 hour. (This dish is not suitable to microwave.)

Sprinkle with cheese, dot with butter and bake 10 minutes more.

Serves 6

CHOUX POTATOES

3 tbsp (45 mL) butter
½ cup (125 mL) water
½ cup (125 mL) flour
3 eggs
4 medium potatoes, cooked and dry
**   mashed**
oil for deep-frying

Bring butter and water to a boil in a pan. Stir in flour and mix well until mixture leaves the side of the pan. Remove from heat and cool.

Place mixture in a bowl and add eggs one at a time, beating well with an electric mixer. Stir in mashed potato.

Heat the oil in a frying pan. Drop 1 tbsp (15 mL) of mixture in oil at a time. Fry until golden brown and drain on paper towels. Serve with any meat or poultry.

Serves 6

TASTY VARIATIONS:
Add any of the following:
☐ ½ cup (60 g) grated strong Cheddar cheese;
☐ ½ cup (125 g) canned corn kernels, drained;
☐ 2 slices bacon, diced and fried.

POTATOES SMITANA

12 small new potatoes, lightly
**   scrubbed**
1 tbsp (15 mL) oil
3 tbsp (45 mL) butter
1 medium onion, diced
1 ¼ cups (310 mL) cream
pepper to taste
juice of 1 lemon
1 tbsp (15 mL) chopped fresh parsley,
**   to garnish**

Add potatoes to boiling water and simmer until tender (or prick potatoes with a fork, place in a covered dish and microwave on HIGH 8 minutes; let stand 2 minutes). Drain and keep warm.

Heat oil and butter in a pan. Add onion and gently fry until transparent. Stir in cream and pepper, bring to a boil and simmer for 5 minutes. Remove from heat and add lemon juice. Pour cream mixture over potatoes and sprinkle with parsley.

Serves 4

TASTY VARIATION:
☐ Replace lemon juice with 3 tbsp (45 mL) sour cream or mayonnaise.

FRENCH POTATO BALLS

4 medium potatoes, peeled, sliced
**   and cooked**
3 tbsp (45 mL) mayonnaise
1 tsp (5 mL) Dijon mustard
1 clove garlic, crushed
1 tbsp (15 mL) chopped fresh parsley
1 tbsp (15 mL) chopped fresh chives
pepper to taste
self-rising flour
2 eggs, beaten with ¼ cup (60 mL)
**   water**
1½–2 cups (375–500 mL) dried bread
**   crumbs**
oil for deep-frying

Mash potatoes with mayonnaise, mustard, garlic, parsley, chives, pepper and sufficient flour to make a firm dough.

Roll potato mixture into balls. Dip each ball into the egg-water mix, then roll in bread crumbs.

Refrigerate coated balls for at least 1 hour. To cook, heat oil and deep-fry balls until brown. Serve with your favorite meal.

Serves 6

Handy hint: When coating food to be fried, always use egg and water, not egg and milk, as milk tends to make food stick to the pan.

TASTY VARIATIONS:
☐ Add 1 tbsp (15 mL) grated cheese;
☐ the potato can be rolled into balls, chilled and fried without the egg and bread crumb coating.

SAUTÉED POTATOES IN LEMON AND GARLIC

4 large potatoes, peeled
3 tbsp (45 mL) oil
4 tbsp (60 mL) butter
grated rind of 1 lemon
juice of 1 lemon
3 tbsp (45 mL) chopped fresh parsley
3 cloves garlic, crushed

Cut potatoes into thin slices, less than ¼ inch (0.6 cm). Cook in boiling water for 4 minutes (or cover with microwave-proof plastic wrap and microwave with 1 tsp (5 mL) water on HIGH 2 minutes). Drain carefully and pat dry with paper towels.

Heat oil and 3 tbsp (45 mL) butter in a heavy-based frying pan. Add enough potatoes to cover bottom of pan and cook, shaking pan so potatoes do not stick. When brown, carefully remove from pan and repeat until all are browned (if necessary add a little more oil and butter).

Combine remaining butter, lemon rind and juice, parsley and garlic in a pan and heat until butter turns a pale brown. Add potatoes and toss until potatoes are well coated.

Serves 4

OIL AND BUTTER
Mixing oil and butter together prevents the butter from burning and removes the oily taste.

Sautéed Potatoes in Lemon and Garlic served with fish

DAUPHINOISE POTATOES

1½ tbsp (20 mL) butter
1 clove garlic, crushed
4 large potatoes, peeled and sliced
1 egg, beaten
3 cups (750 mL) hot milk
1¼ cups (310 mL) Gruyère cheese, grated
pinch nutmeg

Combine butter and garlic and use to grease a casserole dish. Place sliced potatoes in dish. Mix egg, milk and cheese together, and pour over potatoes. Sprinkle with nutmeg. Bake in the oven at 350°F (180°C) for 1¼ hours or until tender. Serve with roasts or barbecued meats.

Serves 6

TASTY VARIATIONS:
☐ Omit cheese and use only 2 cups (500 mL) milk and 1 cup (250 mL) cream;
☐ omit cheese and milk and use 3 cups (750 mL) beef stock instead;
☐ place 4 slices bacon, diced and cooked, on top of potato;
☐ add 1 tbsp (15 mL) diced fresh chives, and top with ½ cup (125 mL) fresh bread crumbs;
☐ in a pan combine 2 tomatoes, sliced, 1 onion, sliced, 1 tbsp (15 mL) oil, 1 clove garlic, crushed, and ½ tsp (2.5 mL) sugar. Fry until tender. Add to egg-milk mixture and pour over potatoes;
☐ mash together canned anchovies with ½ tsp (2.5 mL) each chopped fresh thyme and basil. Add to the egg-milk mixture and pour over potatoes.

1. Combine butter and garlic.

2. Use garlic butter to grease a casserole dish.

3. Layer sliced potatoes in dish.

5. Pour over potatoes, sprinkle with
   nutmeg and bake in the oven.

4. Mix egg, milk and cheese
   together in a bowl.

SPANISH OMELET

¼ cup (60 mL) olive oil
1 large potato, peeled and diced
1 large Spanish onion, finely chopped
5 eggs
freshly ground black pepper

Heat oil in a large frying pan. Sauté potato and onion, stirring occasionally, until both are cooked but not brown. Whisk eggs with pepper and pour into the pan, spreading evenly. Cover pan, lower heat and allow omelet to cook for about 10 minutes.

Place a plate over the frying pan and invert the omelet. Return it immediately to the pan and brown the other side.

Serves 4

POTATO KUGEL

1½ tbsp (20 mL) butter
4 medium potatoes, cooked and dry mashed
4 eggs, beaten
¼ cup (60 mL) potato flour or cornstarch
½ tsp (2.5 mL) baking powder
1 small onion, diced
pepper to taste

Melt butter (or microwave on HIGH 30 seconds) to grease a shallow casserole dish. Combine potatoes and eggs and beat until smooth. Add remaining ingredients and mix well.

Spoon mixture into casserole dish and bake at 350°F (180°C) for 30–35 minutes (or microwave on HIGH 3 minutes, then MEDIUM 8 minutes). Tastes delicious with broiled pork and mushrooms.

Serves 6

TASTY VARIATION:
☐ Sprinkle 3 tbsp (45 mL) grated cheese on top of cooked Kugel and brown under broiler or in oven.

NOMAD POTATOES

4 large potatoes, peeled and thinly sliced
½ cup (125 mL) cream cheese
½ cup (125 mL) milk
1 clove garlic, crushed
3 tbsp (45 mL) Parmesan cheese
1 tbsp (15 mL) chopped fresh chives

Boil potatoes until tender (or arrange in a dish with 1 tsp (5 mL) water, cover with microwave-proof plastic wrap and microwave on HIGH 7 minutes; let stand 2 minutes). Grease a shallow casserole dish and spoon in potatoes.

Beat cream cheese and milk together. Add garlic, pour over potatoes and sprinkle with Parmesan cheese and chives. Bake at 350°F (180°C) for 15 minutes.

Serves 6

TASTY VARIATIONS:
☐ Replace cream cheese with ½ cup (125 mL) cottage cheese;
☐ replace Parmesan cheese with 3 tbsp (45 mL) grated Cheddar.

DRY MASHED
Dry mashed, as the name suggests, refers to the mashing of cooked potatoes without using any butter, milk or cream.

CHAMP

1 onion, sliced
1½ cups (375 mL) milk
¼ cup (60 mL) butter
8 potatoes, cooked
4 green onions, finely diced
pepper to taste

Cook onion in milk for 5 minutes. Add butter and potatoes to onion mixture and mash well. Add diced green onions and pepper. Serve with roasts or broiled meats.

Serves 6

POTATO DUMPLINGS

5 medium potatoes, cooked and mashed
½ tsp (2.5 mL) nutmeg
3 tbsp (45 mL) semolina
¼ cup (60 mL) whole wheat flour
2 eggs, beaten
boiling water
1 cube chicken stock

Combine potatoes, nutmeg, semolina, whole wheat flour and eggs. With floured hands make mixture into balls. Boil water with stock cube and drop in dumplings. Simmer for 10 minutes. Serve with stews or soups.

Serves 6

TASTY VARIATIONS:
☐ Add 1 tbsp (15 mL) chopped fresh chives or parsley and 1 tbsp (15 mL) grated strong Cheddar cheese;
☐ add 1 slice bacon, diced and fried;
☐ dumplings can be cooked in stew or soup the same way as in boiling water.

HASH BROWNS

4 medium potatoes, peeled
3 slices bacon, diced
butter or oil for frying
1 onion, sliced
1 tbsp (15 mL) chopped fresh oregano

Parboil potatoes (or microwave on HIGH 5 minutes). Cut into medium-thick slices. Fry bacon until fat is transparent. Add butter and fry onion and potato with bacon, turning until browned. Sprinkle with oregano.

Serves 6

STUFFINGS
Stuffing should loosely fill chicken as it will expand slightly when cooked.

Potato Dumplings in Golden Nugget Soup

1. Melt butter and add peeled garlic.

2. Stir in hot milk and pepper.
3. Mash potatoes, then combine with sauce.

GARLIC MASHED POTATOES

2 heads of garlic, about 30 cloves
3 tbsp (45 mL) butter
4 large potatoes, peeled
1 tbsp (15 mL) flour
1 cup (250 mL) hot milk
pepper to taste

Separate the garlic cloves and cook in boiling water for 2 minutes; cool and peel.

Melt butter in a heavy-based pan and add peeled garlic. Cover and cook on low heat for 15–20 minutes until tender but not browned. Meanwhile cook potatoes for 20 minutes or until tender (or microwave on HIGH for 6–8 minutes). Remove butter-garlic mixture from heat and stir in flour. Return to heat and cook 1 minute.

Remove from heat again and stir in hot milk and pepper. Bring to a boil and simmer until thickened, stirring all the time. (To microwave, combine garlic, butter and flour in a bowl and microwave on HIGH 1 minute. Stir in hot milk and pepper and microwave on HIGH 3 minutes until mixture boils. Remove from microwave and beat well.)

Push sauce through a sieve or blend until smooth, return to heat and simmer 2 minutes (or microwave on MEDIUM 2 minutes). Drain and mash potatoes, and combine with sauce. Serve with any roast or poultry.

Serves 6

COLCANNON

This is a traditional Irish dish.

2 small cabbages, roughly chopped
2 leeks, diced
1 small onion, diced
4 medium potatoes, cooked and dry mashed
3 tbsp (45 mL) cream
3 tbsp (45 mL) butter
freshly ground black pepper

Boil cabbage, leeks and onion together in a small amount of water until they are tender; drain and mash.

Combine all ingredients and reheat, stirring constantly (or microwave on HIGH 2 minutes). Serve with any meat, fish or poultry.

Serves 4

POTATO CASTLE

1 bunch spinach or Swiss chard, washed
4 medium potatoes, peeled and cooked
3 tbsp (45 mL) butter
milk, to mix
3 tbsp (45 mL) pine nuts
1 clove garlic, crushed
6 hard-boiled eggs, shelled

CHEESE SAUCE
3 tbsp (45 mL) butter
1 tbsp (15 mL) flour
1 cup (250 mL) milk
½ cup (125 mL) grated strong Cheddar cheese

Boil or steam spinach until tender.

To make the Cheese Sauce, melt butter in a pan. Stir in flour and cook 1 minute. Remove from heat and stir in milk. Return to heat and cook until sauce thickens, stirring all the time (or microwave butter on HIGH 30 seconds, add flour and cook on HIGH 1 minute. Stir in milk and cook on HIGH 2 minutes, remove and beat well). Add cheese and stir until melted. Set aside to keep warm.

Mash potatoes with 1½ tbsp (20 mL) butter and enough milk to form a smooth paste. Drain spinach and cut finely. Melt 1½ tbsp (20 mL) butter and gently fry pine nuts and garlic for 1 minute. Add to spinach.

Place spoonfuls of spinach mixture on six dinner plates. Top with a mound of potato. Cut eggs in half. On each plate, arrange two egg halves on top of the potato. Pour Cheese Sauce over potatoes and serve at once.

Serves 6

CARROT AND POTATO CASSEROLE

6 medium potatoes, peeled and sliced
1 onion, sliced
6 tbsp (90 mL) butter
1¼ cups (310 mL) sour cream
1 tsp (5 mL) nutmeg
1 cube chicken stock
4 large carrots, peeled and sliced
1 tbsp (15 mL) milk

Boil potatoes and onion until tender. Drain, reserving 3 tbsp (45 mL) cooking liquid. Mash with 3 tbsp (45 mL) butter, the sour cream and nutmeg. Crumble stock cube over carrots, just cover with water and boil carrots until tender. Drain and mash with reserved 3 tbsp (45 mL) potato cooking liquid.

Spoon half the mashed potato into a greased casserole. Cover with all the mashed carrot, and top with remaining mashed potato. Brush with 1 tbsp (15 mL) milk and dot with 3 tbsp (45 mL) butter. Bake at 350°F (180°C) for approximately 20 minutes or until browned on top. Serve with steaks, roasts and poultry.

Serves 6

BAKED MASHED POTATOES

4 medium potatoes, cooked
1 cup (250 mL) mayonnaise
½ cup (125 mL) sour cream
¼ cup (60 mL) milk
2 eggs, beaten
2 tsp (10 mL) Dijon mustard
¼ cup (60 mL) grated strong Cheddar cheese

Mash potatoes with mayonnaise, sour cream, milk, eggs and mustard.

Spoon into a greased ovenproof dish and top with cheese. Bake at 350°F (180°C) for 20–30 minutes (or microwave on HIGH 7 minutes or until the cheese bubbles). Serve with roasts or chops.

Serves 6

TASTY VARIATIONS:
☐ Replace mayonnaise with 1 cup (250 mL) sour cream and ½ cup (125 mL) milk;
☐ sprinkle 4 slices diced and cooked bacon on top with the cheese.

HAM AND POTATO SCONES

4 medium potatoes, cooked and mashed
4 mushrooms, finely diced
4 slices ham, finely diced
1 onion, finely diced
¼ cup (60 mL) flour
1½ tbsp (20 mL) butter
1 egg, beaten
salt and pepper to taste
oil for frying

Combine all ingredients except oil. Turn onto a floured board and knead until smooth. Roll out like a large sausage. Cut into 10 slices.

Heat oil and fry each slice until browned on both sides. Serve with butter for breakfast.

Serves 6

TASTY VARIATIONS:

Replace ham with:
☐ 1 cup (250 mL) cooked and diced chicken;
☐ 4 slices bacon, diced and lightly cooked;
☐ 3 tbsp (45 mL) grated strong Cheddar cheese.

Replace mushrooms with:
☐ 1 tomato, finely chopped;
☐ ½ green pepper, seeded and diced;
☐ 3 tbsp (45 mL) corn kernels, drained.

Replace onion with:
☐ 2 green onions, diced;
☐ 1 tbsp (15 mL) chopped fresh chives or parsley.

Vegetarian Delights

With the increasing emphasis on health these days, more people are looking for alternatives to meat, chicken and fish. We have included plenty of tasty meatless recipes in this section and throughout the book, to satisfy both your nutritional needs and your taste buds.

POTATO CURRY

¼ cup (60 mL) oil
2 onions, sliced
1 clove garlic, crushed
4 potatoes, peeled and diced
½ tsp (2.5 mL) each: ground turmeric, cumin, cinnamon, cardamom, black pepper, ginger and chili powder
½ tsp (2.5 mL) sugar
1 tbsp (15 mL) coconut milk
1 cup (250 mL) water
1¾ cups (440 mL) canned tomatoes, drained and liquid reserved

ACCOMPANIMENTS
1 cup (250 mL) sour cream or plain yogurt mixed with 1 green cucumber, sliced
4 hard-boiled eggs, crumbled
2 bananas, peeled and sliced, with a squeeze of lemon juice
5 tbsp (75 mL) mango chutney
1 lb (450 g) pineapple pieces, drained
12 pappadums (see Glossary)

Heat oil, add onion and fry until transparent (or microwave on HIGH 2 minutes). Add garlic and potatoes and fry 2 minutes more. Add remaining ingredients, bring to a boil and simmer 30 minutes or until potato is cooked.

Serve curry with rice and accompaniments in separate bowls.

Serves 6

Handy hint: Leaving a metal spoon in a saucepan of simmering rice prevents water from boiling over.

TASTY VARIATIONS:
☐ With onions fry 2 eggplants, diced, salted and washed;
☐ 1 bunch spinach or Swiss chard, washed, shredded and cooked until tender. Add after 30 minutes of cooking;
☐ With onions fry 4 zucchini, diced and 2 green onions, diced;
☐ 1 lb (450 g) lima beans (fresh or frozen) and 2 carrots, peeled and diced. Cook with potatoes.

OLD WIVES' TALES
Rub a raw potato on a wart, then bury the potato; as the potato rots so the wart will go.

Wrap grated potatoes on frostbite or burns.

Wrap a raw grated potato in a cloth and place over the eyes for 15 minutes; this is said to remove wrinkles.

Wrap a slice of baked potato in a stocking and tie around the throat to cure sore throats and rheumatism.

Write the name of an enemy on a piece of paper, stick it into a potato and the victim will die within the month.

Use the water from a boiled potato to cure a sprain.

Potato Curry served with traditional accompaniments – boiled rice, crispy pappadums, sliced banana, diced cucumber and yogurt

POTATO FLAPJACKS

These make an ideal breakfast served with eggs, bacon or sausage.

1 egg
1 cup (250 mL) flour
2 cups (500 mL) milk
6 medium potatoes, peeled and grated
¼ cup (60 mL) oil

Combine egg, flour and milk in a blender; process for 30 seconds. Add potatoes 1 tbsp (15 mL) at a time and blend until smooth. Heat a little oil in a pan and pour in 1 tbsp (15 mL) of potato mixture, 4 tbsp (60 mL) for large flapjacks. Move the pan to spread mixture over base. Fry both sides until brown and crisp.

Serves 6

CHEESE AND POTATO FRITTERS

1 cup (250 mL) self-rising flour
1 cup (250 mL) grated strong Cheddar cheese
1 onion, grated
4 medium potatoes, peeled and grated
2 eggs, beaten
1 tsp (5 mL) nutmeg
½ cup (125 mL) evaporated milk
oil for deep-frying
chutney, to serve

In a bowl combine all ingredients except for oil and chutney, and beat well to make a thick batter. Let stand for 5 minutes. Heat oil and drop in batter, 1 tbsp (15 mL) at a time. Cook both sides until golden. Serve with a spoonful of chutney as an accompaniment to roasts.

Serves 6

TASTY VARIATIONS:
☐ Add 3 tbsp (45 mL) canned corn kernels and 1 tbsp (15 mL) diced green pepper;
☐ 1 carrot, peeled and grated, and 2 green onions, diced;
☐ ¼ tsp (1 mL) each ground chili powder, cumin, turmeric and 2 tsp (10 mL) lemon juice.

POTATOES AND YOGURT

An ideal accompaniment to roast lamb.

3 tbsp (45 mL) oil
12 tiny new potatoes, washed and sliced
pinch ground cloves
½ tsp (2.5 mL) ground cinnamon
2 bay leaves
½ tsp (2.5 mL) crushed fresh ginger root
3 tbsp (45 mL) chopped mixed fresh herbs
¾ cup (180 mL) plain yogurt

Heat oil in frying pan. Add new potatoes, cloves, cinnamon, bay leaves and ginger root. Stir-fry for 2 minutes, then stir in herbs and yogurt and heat through without boiling. Remove bay leaves and serve in an attractive bowl.

Serves 6

Note: Crush ginger root in a garlic press.

ARABIAN MIXED VEGETABLES

3 tbsp (45 mL) oil or butter
1 onion, sliced
1 bay leaf
1 tbsp (15 mL) chopped fresh dill
½ stalk celery, finely diced
1 potato, peeled and diced
1 carrot, peeled and diced
1 green apple, cored and diced
2 tomatoes, diced
2 small zucchini, diced
¼ cauliflower, divided into florets

Heat oil in pan, add onion and fry until transparent. Add all herbs and vegetables. Stir-fry for 2 minutes, lower heat and simmer for 10 minutes (or microwave, replacing oil with butter, on HIGH 4 minutes).

To serve, remove bay leaf and place in a serving bowl.

Serves 6

TASTY VARIATIONS:
☐ Add 1½ tbsp (20 mL) raisins;
☐ 1½ tbsp (20 mL) nuts.

VEGETARIAN PIE

1 cup (250 mL) red lentils
½ cup (125 mL) chick peas
2 cups (500 mL) water
2 cubes vegetable stock
1 tbsp (15 mL) oil or butter
2 onions, sliced
1 clove garlic, crushed
¼ lb (110 g) green beans, sliced
1 red pepper, seeded and diced
1½ cups (325 mL) tomato purée or
sauce
1 tbsp (15 mL) Worcestershire sauce
1 tbsp (15 mL) tomato paste
pinch dried oregano
pepper to taste
3 medium potatoes, cooked and
mashed
3 tbsp (45 mL) chopped fresh parsley
3 tbsp (45 mL) milk
3 tbsp (45 mL) butter
paprika

Pour water over lentils and chick peas, cover and soak overnight. Drain well.

Cook chick peas in water with crumbled stock cubes for 30 minutes, then add lentils and cook 30 minutes more, or until tender. Drain and set aside.

Heat oil, add onions and gently fry until transparent. Add garlic, beans, red pepper and stir-fry for 2 minutes (or combine butter instead of oil, onions, garlic, beans and red pepper and microwave on HIGH 2 minutes).

Add tomato purée, Worcestershire sauce, tomato paste and the seasonings. Bring to a boil and simmer for 2 minutes (or microwave on HIGH 2 minutes). Spoon lentils and peas into a greased casserole dish and add tomato mixture.

Combine mashed potatoes with parsley, milk and butter, and spread over tomato mixture. Sprinkle with a little paprika and bake at 350°F (180°C) for 20 minutes (or microwave on HIGH 4 minutes). Serve warm with salad and crusty bread.

Serves 6

TASTY VARIATION:

☐ Top with grated cheese and bake until brown (or microwave until cheese bubbles).

GNOCCHI WITH CHEDDAR CHEESE SAUCE

3 medium potatoes, peeled and sliced
2 eggs, beaten
1½ cups (325 mL) flour

CHEDDAR CHEESE SAUCE
3 tbsp (45 mL) butter
1 tbsp (15 mL) flour
1 cup (250 mL) milk
1 cup (250 mL) grated strong Cheddar
cheese
1 tsp (5 mL) dry mustard

Boil potatoes until tender. Drain, reserving water in pan. Mash potatoes well with eggs. Add flour and mix to a dry dough. Turn out onto a floured board and knead well until smooth (about 2 minutes).

Divide mixture into four. Roll each piece into a sausage shape and cut into 1 inch (2.5 cm) slices. Press gently against a grater or a fork to roughen the surface. Add 1 cup (250 mL) extra water to the reserved water in the pan and bring to a boil. Drop gnocchi a few at a time into the boiling water — they will drop to the bottom then rise. Boil for 1 minute after gnocchi rises to top of pan, then remove from pan with a slotted spoon. Drain on paper towels.

To make sauce, melt butter in a pan, stir in flour and cook for 1 minute. Remove from heat and stir in milk. Return to heat and stir until mixture boils and thickens. (Alternatively, microwave butter on HIGH 30 seconds then stir in flour, cook on HIGH 1 minute. Add milk, stir and cook on HIGH 2 minutes then beat well.)

Add cheese and mustard and stir until cheese melts. To serve, place cooked gnocchi in a greased casserole dish. Pour sauce over gnocchi and brown under broiler (or microwave on HIGH until cheese bubbles).

> STORAGE
> Store potatoes in a dark, cool spot in brown paper bags. New potatoes are best kept in the refrigerator, also in paper bags as the paper absorbs moisture.

Gnocchi with Cheddar Cheese Sauce

BIRD'S NEST

**1¾ lbs (800 g) broccoli or 1 lb (450 g)
 fresh spinach (or Swiss chard)
 leaves
7 tbsp (105 mL) butter
1 clove garlic, crushed
3 tbsp (45 mL) flour
1 cup (250 mL) milk
6 eggs, separated
12 tiny new potatoes, washed
 (see Note)
¼ cup (60 mL) chopped fresh mint
 or parsley
Parmesan cheese, to serve**

Soak broccoli or spinach in warm water
(see Note) for 5 minutes. Shake well and
boil for 10 minutes. Drain and mash broccoli or cut spinach very finely. Preheat
oven to 350°F (180°C).

Melt 4 tbsp (60 mL) butter in a pan, add
garlic and gently fry but do not allow to
brown. Stir in flour and cook for 1 minute.
Remove from heat and stir in milk. Return
to heat and allow to boil and thicken, stirring all the time.

(Alternatively, microwave butter and
garlic on HIGH 30 seconds, stir in flour
and cook on HIGH 1 minute. Add milk
and cook on HIGH 2 minutes, remove
and beat well.)

Beat in egg yolks and add broccoli.
Whisk egg whites until stiff and whisk into
vegetable mixture. Spoon mixture into a
greased 8 inch (20 cm) ring pan. Stand
pan in a baking dish with 1 inch (2.5 cm)
warm water and bake for 45 minutes.

Boil new potatoes until tender (or
microwave potatoes, covered and with
1 tsp (5 mL) water, on HIGH 6 minutes).

Melt remaining 3 tbsp (45 mL) butter in
a pan (or microwave on HIGH 30 seconds). Add chopped mint and new potatoes and toss until coated. Place in a
covered dish in oven to keep warm.

When soufflé is cooked, place a large
serving dish on top of the ring pan, carefully turn the plate over and gently turn
out soufflé.

Fill center with new potatoes and sprinkle with Parmesan cheese. Serve with
crusty bread and tomato.

Serves 6

Note: Warm water draws out any dirt and
insects in broccoli and spinach.

1 lb (450 g) canned potatoes are ideal
for this recipe. Drain and wash in warm
water, as there is no need to cook them.

1. Melt butter and garlic; stir in milk.

2. Beat in egg yolks and broccoli; add stiffened egg whites.

3. Spoon into a greased ring pan and stand pan in water.

4. When cooked, place a serving dish on top of ring pan and invert.

5. Fill center with potatoes and sprinkle with Parmesan.

61

Tomato Cream Soup

GOLDEN NUGGET SOUP

6 very small sugar pumpkins, washed
2 medium potatoes, peeled and sliced
1 onion, sliced
2 cups (500 mL) water
½ cup (125 mL) cream
croutons, to serve

Slice the top off each pumpkin, scoop out the seeds and pour 1 tbsp (15 mL) water into each pumpkin. Bake at 350°F (180°C) until the insides are tender (or microwave on HIGH 15 minutes). Combine potatoes and onion in a pan, add water, bring to a boil and simmer for 30 minutes.

Cool pumpkins slightly, remove pulp and add to the potato soup. Heat shells in the oven at 350°F (180°C) for 10 minutes (or microwave on HIGH 2 minutes just before serving). Blend or push soup through a sieve. Reheat but do not boil (or microwave on HIGH 5 minutes).

To serve, spoon soup into pumpkin shells. Swirl in cream. Put pumpkins in a bowl if they need steadying, and serve with a bowl of croutons.

Serves 6

CARROT SOUP

¼ cup (60 mL) butter
2 onions, sliced
2 large potatoes, peeled and sliced
2 stalks celery, diced
4 carrots, peeled and sliced
4 cups (1 L) water
1 tsp (5 mL) sugar
1 clove garlic, crushed
pepper to taste
½ cup (125 mL) cream

Melt butter, add onions and fry until transparent. Add potatoes, celery and carrots and fry for 1 minute more. Add water, sugar, garlic and pepper. Bring to a boil, lower heat and simmer for 30 minutes.

Blend or push through a sieve. Reheat (or microwave on HIGH 5 minutes). Serve in a tureen or soup bowls with a swirl of cream on top.

Serves 6

TASTY VARIATION:
☐ Replace carrots with 6 zucchinis, sliced, or 3 lbs (1.5 kg) pumpkin.

POTATO PEEL STOCK

This recipe can be used to replace water in all the soup recipes in this book. Prepare it when next peeling potatoes.

washed potato peels of 6 potatoes
1 onion, sliced
2 carrots, peeled and sliced
1 stalk celery, diced
5 cups (1.25 L) water

Combine all ingredients in a pot and bring to a boil. Lower heat and simmer for 1½ hours. As the water evaporates, add a little more to keep the vegetables covered.

Strain and discard vegetables. Store stock in refrigerator or freeze until required.

Makes 4 cups (1 L)

TASTY VARIATION:
☐ Serve the stock as soup. Discard potato peels only and serve.

TOMATO CREAM SOUP

2 leeks
3 tbsp (45 mL) butter
1 lb (450 g) tomatoes, peeled and
** roughly chopped**
3 large potatoes, peeled and sliced
1 tsp (5 mL) sugar
2½ cups (625 mL) water
½ cup (125 mL) sour cream
chopped fresh parsley and croutons,
** to serve**

Finely slice only the white part of the leek. Melt butter, add leek and gently fry for 1 minute. Remove from heat and add chopped tomatoes. Return to heat, stirring until tomatoes soften. Add potatoes, sugar and water and bring to a boil. Lower heat and simmer for 30 minutes.

Blend until smooth. Stir in cream and carefully reheat (or pour into a bowl and microwave on MEDIUM until soup steams). Do not allow soup to boil as the cream will curdle. Serve with a sprinkle of parsley and a few croutons.

Serves 4

POTATO AND AVOCADO SOUP

3 cups (750 mL) water
2 cubes vegetable stock
2 large potatoes, peeled and sliced
3 onions, sliced
2 ripe avocados, peeled and sliced
2 tsp (10 mL) lemon juice
1¼ cups (310 mL) cream
2 tsp (10 mL) nutmeg

Combine water, crumbled stock cubes, potatoes and onions in a pan and bring to a boil. Lower heat and simmer for 30 minutes. Blend until smooth.

Blend or purée avocados with lemon juice and ½ cup (125 mL) of potato liquid.

Heat both soups in separate pans (or microwave on HIGH 4 minutes). Stir cream into the avocado soup. Pour the soups into separate jugs. Holding a jug in each hand, pour soups into individual bowls at the same time, then gently swirl with a knife. Sprinkle with nutmeg.

Serves 6

TASTY VARIATION:

☐ Replace avocado soup with 2½ cups (625 mL) Carrot Soup (see recipe).

POTATO SAMBAL

4 medium potatoes, peeled and diced
2 green chili peppers, diced
½ tsp (2.5 mL) chili powder
½ onion, finely diced
1 tsp (5 mL) olive oil
juice of ½ lemon
Poori (see recipe), to serve

Boil potatoes until tender (or microwave with 1 tsp (5 mL) water on HIGH 8 minutes). Combine with all remaining ingredients and serve with Poori (see recipe).

Serves 6 as a side dish

POORI

3¼ cups (810 mL) white or whole
**   wheat flour**
cold water
extra flour
½ cup (125 mL) unsalted butter

Sift flour, add sufficient cold water to make a stiff dough. Cover with a damp cloth and leave for 1 hour. Knead with a little extra flour until smooth and shape into small balls. Heat butter in a pan and put in one ball at a time, pressing balls flat with a spatula. Cook both sides until balls puff up. Drain on paper towels and serve at once.

Serves 6

DAHIN ALOO

Dahin is Indian for yogurt and Aloo means potatoes. For a truly exotic touch, serve this Indian specialty with pappadums.

¼ cup (60 mL) ghee or unsalted butter
1 onion, sliced
1 tsp (5 mL) peeled and finely sliced
**   fresh ginger root**
1 red chili pepper, finely chopped
1 tbsp (15 mL) ground coriander
1 tsp (5 mL) ground turmeric
pinch mace
2 tomatoes, peeled and chopped
¾ cup (180 mL) plain yogurt
1 tsp (5 mL) sugar
¼ cup (60 mL) raisins
6 potatoes, peeled, cooked and sliced
pappadums, to serve

Heat butter or ghee in a pan. Add onion and ginger and fry until onion is transparent. Add chili pepper, spices, tomatoes, yogurt and sugar. Simmer until thick. Add raisins and potatoes and heat through. Serve with pappadums.

Serves 6

DOSA WITH POTATO STUFFING

1½ cups (325 mL) rice flour
1½ cups (325 mL) flour
½ tsp (2.5 mL) chili powder, or more
**   to taste**
3 tbsp (45 mL) plain yogurt
1½ tbsp (20 mL) unsalted butter
water, to mix
oil for frying

STUFFING
1½ tbsp (20 mL) ghee or unsalted
**   butter**
1 onion, finely diced
¼ tsp (1 mL) mustard seeds
¼ tsp (1 mL) ground turmeric
¼ tsp (1 mL) chili powder
2 potatoes, peeled, diced and cooked

Combine flours, chili powder, yogurt, butter and sufficient water to make a thick batter. Cover with damp cloth and let stand overnight at room temperature.

Next day, heat oil and pour in 1 tbsp (15 mL) batter at a time. Fry both sides until golden. Repeat until all the mixture is used. Set dosa aside and keep warm.

To make stuffing, heat ghee or butter in pan and fry onion until transparent. Add all seasonings and potatoes and heat through. Spoon a little mixture into the center of each dosa and fold. Serve with roasts or chicken curry.

Serves 6

TASTY VARIATIONS:

☐ Replace onion with 2 green chili peppers, and seasonings with garam masala;
☐ add ½ lb (225 g) fresh green peas, cooked, and 2 green onions, diced.

EGGPLANT AND POTATO BAKE

2 eggplants
salt
4 medium potatoes, peeled and sliced
1 tbsp (15 mL) oil or butter
2 onions, sliced
1 cup (250 mL) grated cheese

Slice eggplants and sprinkle with salt. Let stand 30 minutes then rinse under cold water. Cook potatoes until tender (or microwave with 2 tsp (10 mL) water on HIGH 8 minutes, let stand 3 minutes). Drain on paper towels.

Heat oil, add onions and fry until transparent (or microwave onions, using butter in place of oil, on HIGH 2 minutes). Grease a casserole dish and arrange eggplant slices as a base. Sprinkle lightly with cheese, cover with a layer of potato, top with onion and a little more cheese. Repeat until all vegetables are used, finishing with cheese.

Cover dish and bake at 350°F (180°C) for 1¼ hours. Remove lid and bake 15 minutes more. Serve as a main meal or as a side dish with broiled meat.

Serves 6

TASTY VARIATIONS:
Add any of the following:
☐ 2 tomatoes, sliced;
☐ 2 carrots, peeled and sliced;
☐ 2 zucchini, sliced;
☐ combine 2 eggs, ½ cup (125 mL) milk, pinch nutmeg, pour over vegetables, then top with remaining cheese and bake;
☐ top with 3 lbs (1.5 kg) mashed pumpkin combined with 1 egg white, whisked, then sprinkle with remaining cheese and bake.

EGGPLANTS
Sprinkling salt on sliced eggplant takes away the bitter juices. Don't forget to rinse the eggplants and drain before using.

Fabulous Fries

Diets notwithstanding, most of us love the occasional excursion into fried foods, and they are often family favorites. Potato chips, French fries, croquettes, crispy potatoes, pommes noisettes — homemade is infinitely superior to packaged foods. Eaten in moderation, say once a week, they shouldn't damage your health or your waistline.

PERUVIAN BALLS IN SPICY PEANUT SAUCE

3 tbsp (45 mL) butter
2 onions, sliced
4 large potatoes, cooked and dry mashed
2 cups (500 mL) Munster cheese, grated
oil for shallow-frying

SPICY PEANUT SAUCE
⅓ cup (80 mL) oil or butter
1 onion, grated
1¼ cups (325 mL) raw, shelled peanuts or 1 cup (250 mL) peanut butter
2 chili peppers, finely diced
3 cloves garlic, crushed
½ cup (125 mL) warm water
1 tbsp (15 mL) brown sugar
1 tbsp (15 mL) soy sauce
3 tbsp (45 mL) lemon juice

Melt butter, add onions and gently fry until transparent (or microwave butter and onions on HIGH 2 minutes). Combine with potatoes and cheese. Divide into 12 balls, flattening each slightly with the back of a tablespoon. Chill until ready to use.

To make sauce, heat oil, add onion and fry until transparent (or substitute butter for oil and microwave on HIGH 2 minutes). In a blender combine onion with all remaining sauce ingredients and process until smooth. Pour purée into a pan, bring to a boil and simmer for 3 minutes to thicken.

Heat oil in a frying pan and fry flattened balls on both sides until golden. Serve with Spicy Peanut Sauce. This dish goes well with roast chicken and green salad.

Serves 6

PARATHAS

2 cups (500 mL) flour
2 cups (500 mL) whole wheat flour
3 tbsp (45 mL) butter
1 cup (250 mL) warm water
oil for frying

FILLING
2 medium potatoes, cooked and dry mashed
1 cup (250 mL) grated Cheddar cheese
2 tsp (10 mL) curry powder

Sift flours together in a bowl. Rub in butter with fingertips. Stir in water with a knife and mix to a firm dough. Turn out onto a floured board and knead until smooth. Cover and let stand for 10 minutes.

Divide dough into six portions. Roll each section into a circle approximately ½ inch (1 cm) in diameter.

Combine filling ingredients. Place a spoonful of filling in the center of each circle and then roll into a ball. Flatten with a rolling pin into 4 inch (10 cm) circles.

Heat oil in a frying pan and fry flattened balls on both sides until golden. Serve with Spicy Peanut Sauce. This dish goes well with roast chicken and green salad.

Serves 6

BULGUR POTATO BALLS

1 cup (250 mL) bulgur
6 medium potatoes, cooked and dry mashed
1 cup (250 mL) flour
pepper to taste

FILLING
2 onions, sliced
3 tbsp (45 mL) water
¼ tsp (1 mL) ground allspice
¼ cup (60 mL) pine nuts
¼ cup (60 mL) currants or raisins
3 tbsp (45 mL) tahini
oil for deep-frying

Place bulgur in a bowl and cover with water. Soak for 5 minutes, then drain, pressing with a spoon to remove water. Combine mashed potatoes, bulgur, flour and pepper.

To make the filling, place onions in a pan with the water. Boil for 10 minutes then drain (or microwave onions with 2 tsp (10 mL) water on HIGH 4 minutes). Add all filling ingredients to onions, stirring well to combine.

Take one tbsp (15 mL) of cracked wheat mixture and roll into a ball in your hand. Flatten out, place a spoonful of filling in the center, then reshape into a ball. Repeat until both mixtures are used. Heat oil and fry balls until golden. Serve as appetizers with drinks.

Serves 6

Note: Bulgur is a processed cracked wheat, available at supermarkets, delicatessens and health food stores. It is also known as bulkar (Arabic), pourgouri (Greek) and bular (Turkish). Tahini is a paste made from crushed sesame seeds. It can be bought in health food shops and some delicatessens.

FRYING
There are 3 types of frying:
☐ shallow-frying, which is ideal for leftovers and uses approximately 1 inch (2.5 cm) of heated oil in a pan;
☐ pan-frying, a delicious way of cooking leftovers or thinly sliced potatoes in approximately 1 tbsp (15 mL) of heated oil in a pan;
☐ deep-frying, which is for cooking or reheating and uses hot oil in a deep fryer.

Peruvian Balls in Spicy Peanut Sauce

PERFECT FRENCH FRIES

The French fry was originally known as the 'Saratoga Chip'. It was invented by an Indian cook with the unlikely name of George Crumb, in Saratoga. He finely sliced the potato and then quickly fried it in hot fat.

**6 medium potatoes, peeled and
    washed
oil for deep frying
salt (optional)**

Slice potatoes into thin strips. Place in a bowl of ice water for at least 10 minutes, preferably 1–2 hours. Drain and dry well on paper towels.

Heat the oil to 375°F (190°C). Place potato strips in a frying basket and lower carefully into the hot oil. Fry for 5–8 minutes, then remove and drain. At this point, the fries are blanched and can stand for several hours until ready for the final cooking. (Once blanched, they can be refrigerated, covered, for up to 4 hours, then fried and served.)

Increase oil temperature to 400°F (200°C) and cook fries for the second time until they are crisp and golden (about 3–5 minutes). Drain on paper towels and serve at once.

Serves 4

1. Soak uncooked fries in ice water for at least 10 minutes.

FRENCH FRIES
Another story says French fries were created in France by Antonine Parmentier, who served them at a dinner in honor of Benjamin Franklin. Franklin cannot have been too impressed, as it was left to Thomas Jefferson to introduce them to America at a White House dinner.

French fries or chips?
In some countries, French fries are called "chips." In Australia, for instance, thick French fries are called chips and thin ones are called fries. In Britain, French fries are called fries or chips, and potato chips are called "crisps." In Canada, just to confuse the issue, chips are potato chips in some parts of the country; on the east coast, however, chips are French fries.

2. Blanch fries 5–8 minutes.

3. Drain well on paper towels.

WHICH OIL?

Oil is a refined liquid made from extracts of seeds, nuts, fruits and occasionally animal fats. Cooking oils have been processed to be relatively flavorless, odorless and to keep for a period of time. They are divided into five groups:

Delicate, aromatic oils (e.g. sesame, walnut, grape)
These oils should be always stored in the refrigerator. Use sparingly in salads and for stir-frying.

Polyunsaturated oils (e.g. sunflower, safflower, corn and some blended oils)
Believed to help control blood fats, these oils can be used in deep or shallow-frying, as they have a good tolerance to high temperatures.

Mono-unsaturated (e.g. peanut, olive and sesame)
These oils break down at high temperatures and should not be used for deep-frying. They have an excellent flavor for salads. If the flavor is too strong, reduce by mixing an equal quantity of polyunsaturated oil. Olive oil, particularly virgin olive oil, is excellent for salads.

Saturated oils (e.g. coconut and animal oils)
These oils are very strong and not really recommended for general cooking.

Solidified oils
These are processed to make them solid at room temperature. They are slightly cheaper and are recommended for deep and shallow frying. Available from supermarkets. Used and unused oils should never be mixed. Buy only sufficient oil to be used within two months. Oils may be used several times, strained and stored (except for aromatic oils) in a tightly sealed container away from light.

CAUTION: If you overheat your oil and it begins to smoke, this is a sign that the oil has started to break down and should be discarded. The smoky taste will penetrate the food, and at this stage the oil can easily burst into flames.

4. Fry for the second time until golden, 3–5 minutes.

BAKED SALMON CROQUETTES WITH QUICK TOMATO SAUCE

1 lb (450 g) canned salmon, drained
1 onion, diced
2 eggs, beaten
3 tbsp (45 mL) mayonnaise
1 tbsp (15 mL) chopped fresh parsley
2 medium potatoes, cooked and dry mashed
1 tbsp (15 mL) water
1½ – 2 cups (325-500 mL) dried bread crumbs
1 tbsp (15 mL) grated Parmesan cheese

TOMATO SAUCE
⅓ cup (85 mL) tomato sauce
1 onion, diced
½ cube chicken stock
1 tbsp (15 mL) water

Remove bones from salmon and crumble fish into a bowl. Combine with onion, 1 egg, mayonnaise, parsley and mashed potatoes. Take spoonfuls and mold into croquette shapes (oval). Refrigerate for 1 hour.

Mix the other egg with water and, in another bowl mix bread crumbs with cheese. Dip croquettes into egg mixture then toss in bread crumb and cheese mixture. Refrigerate a further 1 hour.

Arrange croquettes in a greased baking dish and bake at 350°F (180°C) for 15 – 20 minutes.

Mix sauce ingredients together in a pan and bring to a boil (or microwave on HIGH 2 minutes). Remove from heat, stir well and pour into a gravy boat.

Serves 6

TASTY VARIATIONS:
☐ For a delicious meal serve with French fries and a green salad;
☐ add a dash of Worcestershire or Tabasco sauce to tingle the taste buds.

CHEESE CROQUETTES WITH MUSTARD SAUCE

2 medium potatoes, cooked
3 tbsp (45 mL) butter
1 egg yolk
3 tbsp (45 mL) milk
⅔ cup (175 mL) grated strong Cheddar cheese
3 tbsp (45 mL) chopped fresh parsley
1 egg, beaten
3 tbsp (45 mL) water
1½ – 2 cups (325-500 mL) dried bread crumbs
3 tbsp (45 mL) almond halves
oil for deep frying

SAUCE
3 tbsp (45 mL) butter
1 tbsp (15 mL) flour
¼ cup (60 mL) water
¼ cup (60 mL) cream
2 tsp (10 mL) Dijon mustard

Mash potatoes with butter, egg yolk, milk, cheese and parsley. Take tablespoonfuls (15 mL) of mixture and form into croquette shapes (oval); chill for 1 hour. Mix egg and water together. Dip croquettes in egg-water mixture, then bread crumbs, then press an almond half in each. Chill for a further 1 hour.

To make sauce, melt butter and stir in flour. Cook 1 minute, then remove from heat and stir in water, cream and mustard. Return to heat and stir until sauce boils and thickens.

(Alternatively, microwave butter on HIGH 1 minute, add flour and cook on HIGH 1 minute. Stir in water, cream and mustard and cook on MEDIUM 2 minutes. Remove and stir well.)

Heat oil and deep-fry croquettes until golden. Drain on paper towels. To serve, arrange croquettes on plates, pour sauce over croquettes and serve with roasts or fish.

Serves 6

SMOKED FISH CAKES WITH TARTAR SAUCE

½ lb (225 g) potatoes, mashed
8 oz (225 g) canned smoked fish, flaked
salt and pepper to taste
pinch ground nutmeg
1 tbsp (15 mL) finely chopped fresh parsley
1 tbsp (15 mL) lemon juice
1 egg, beaten
dried bread crumbs, to coat

TARTAR SAUCE
1 cup (250 mL) mayonnaise
3 tbsp (45 mL) chopped gherkins or dill pickles
1 tbsp (15 mL) capers
finely chopped fresh parsley, to taste

Combine mashed potatoes with all remaining fish cake ingredients. Shape into small balls, dip in beaten egg and coat with bread crumbs.

Heat oil in a pan until hot, 375°F (190°C). Fry cakes until golden on both sides. Drain on paper towels and serve with sauce.

To make sauce, combine all sauce ingredients in a bowl and mix. Store in a well-sealed glass jar. Will keep refrigerated for up to ten days.

Serves 4

POMMES DE TERRE BERNY

4 large potatoes, cooked and dry mashed
2 eggs
3 tbsp (45 mL) cream
3 tbsp (45 mL) self-rising flour
3 tbsp (45 mL) all-purpose flour
3 tbsp (45 mL) water
1½ cups (375 mL) flaked almonds
oil for deep frying

Combine mashed potatoes with 1 egg, cream and self-rising flour. Mix well. If mixture is too soft, add extra flour. Place all-purpose flour in a plastic bag. Drop in spoonfuls of potato mixture and toss until lightly covered with flour. Remove and roll into balls.

Mix the other egg with the water. Dip potato balls in egg-water mixture then roll in flaked almonds. Chill until ready to use. Heat oil and fry balls until golden (the almonds will brown quickly). Serve with roasts or fish.

Serves 6

TASTY VARIATIONS:
Add to the potato mixture any of the following:
☐ 1 clove garlic, crushed;
☐ 1 tbsp (15 mL) grated Parmesan cheese;
☐ 1 tbsp (15 mL) chopped fresh parsley;
☐ 1 small onion, finely diced;
☐ replace cream with 3 tbsp (45 mL) sour cream; replace almonds with 2 cups (500 mL) dried bread crumbs.

CRISPY POTATOES

4 large potatoes, peeled, washed and diced
½ cup (125 mL) oil for shallow-frying

Pat potatoes dry with paper towels. Heat oil in a pan and add potatoes, stirring until tender.

Serves 6

CORN AND POTATO PUFFS

11 oz (310 g) canned corn kernels, drained
1 egg, beaten
3 tbsp (45 mL) flour
4 medium potatoes, cooked and dry mashed
3 tbsp (45 mL) chutney
3 tbsp (45 mL) plain yogurt
1 red pepper, seeded and finely diced
4 green onions, finely diced
2 cloves garlic, crushed
oil for deep frying

In a bowl, combine drained corn with beaten egg, flour, mashed potatoes, chutney, yogurt, red pepper, green onions and garlic. Heat oil in a pan and fry spoonfuls of mixture until golden. Drain on paper towels and serve with roasts, or for breakfast with eggs and bacon.

TASTY VARIATIONS:
Add to the mixture any of the following:
☐ 1 tbsp (15 mL) grated Parmesan cheese;
☐ 1 tbsp (15 mL) peas, cooked, or carrots, diced and cooked;
☐ 1 tbsp (15 mL) bacon, diced and cooked.

POMMES NOISETTES

4 medium potatoes, peeled and washed
½ tsp (2.5 mL) salt
cold water
¼ cup (60 mL) butter

With a melon baller, scoop potato into balls. Place in salted cold water (make sure the potato balls are covered with water to prevent browning). Cover with a lid and let stand for 1 hour, then drain.

Boil a large pot of water and cook potatoes 15 minutes (or microwave on HIGH approximately 5 minutes until tender). Drain and pat dry with paper towels. Melt butter in a pan and allow to foam. Add potatoes and stir until golden brown.

Serves 6

POTATO SCALLOPS

4 large potatoes, peeled and thinly sliced
flour, to dust
oil for deep frying

BATTER 1
1 tbsp (15 mL) flour
1 cup (250 mL) self-rising flour
water

BATTER 2
1 cup (250 mL) self-rising flour
6 oz (180 mL) beer
flour, to dust

Dust potato slices with flour and heat oil in a deep-fryer.

To make batter 1, place flours in a bowl and whisk in sufficient water to make a smooth batter. To make batter 2, place self-rising flour in a bowl and whisk in enough beer for a smooth batter.

Dip potato slices into batter of your choice. If using batter 2, dust slices with flour after dipping. Fry in hot oil until light brown. Drain on paper towels. Just before serving, reheat oil and refry until golden; drain.

Serves 6

MOCK FISH CAKES

2 large potatoes, peeled, washed and grated
1 tbsp (15 mL) self-rising flour (see Note)
1 egg, beaten
water, to mix
oil for shallow-frying
cooked bacon strips
tomato sauce or catsup, to serve

Place grated potatoes in a bowl. Add flour, egg and sufficient water to bind together. Heat oil and drop tablespoonfuls (15 mL) of mixture into pan. Flatten with the back of a spatula. Cook both sides until golden and drain on paper towels.

To serve, accompany with strips of bacon or a little tomato sauce or catsup.

Serves 6

Note: If preparing this recipe ahead of time, use plain flour.

TASTY VARIATIONS:
☐ Add 1 small onion, grated, to the mixture before cooking;
☐ Add 1 tbsp (15 mL) chopped fresh parsley or chives before cooking.

Pommes Noisettes and Corn and Potato Puffs

Fillings, Toppings and Stuffings

The versatile potato can form the basis for poultry stuffings or can be used to make luscious fillings for potato cups, or served with a variety of quick, easy toppings.

HERB STUFFING FOR CHICKEN

2 medium potatoes, cooked and dry mashed
3 onions, sliced
3 tbsp (45 mL) butter
1 tbsp (15 mL) fresh sage
pepper to taste
1 egg
1 tbsp (15 mL) chopped fresh thyme

Combine all ingredients and use to stuff a 3 lb (1.5 kg) chicken.

TASTY VARIATIONS:
Add or substitute any of the following:
☐ 4 fried chopped mushrooms;
☐ 3 tbsp (45 mL) corn kernels;
☐ 2 slices bacon, diced and cooked;
☐ 2 stalks celery, diced.

ONION STUFFING

⅓ cup (85 mL) butter
2 onions, diced
½ lb (225 g) sausages or sausage meat
1 large potato, cooked and dry mashed
1 egg
pepper to taste
3 tbsp (45 mL) chopped fresh parsley

Heat butter in a pan. Add onions and gently fry until transparent (or combine butter and onion in a dish, microwave on HIGH 2 minutes). Remove onion with a slotted spoon. Remove sausage meat from casings and mix thoroughly in a bowl with onion, cooked potato, egg, pepper and parsley. Use for stuffing a 4 lb (2 kg) chicken or other poultry.

ROAST CHICKEN

3 lb (1.5 kg) chicken
3 tbsp (45 mL) oil or butter

Preheat oven to 375°F (190°C). Fill cavity of chicken with the stuffing of your choice. Place chicken in a roasting pan with oil and roast for 1½ – 2 hours, basting frequently. If chicken sticks to the bottom of the pan, add more oil or butter.

Serves 4

FRUITY STUFFING

¼ cup (60 mL) butter
1 large onion, finely chopped
12 dried apricots, chopped
6 prunes, pitted and chopped
¼ cup (60 mL) raisins
¼ cup (60 mL) currants
1 large apple, cored and diced
½ tsp (2.5 mL) salt
¼ tsp (1 mL) pepper
¼ tsp (1 mL) ground cinnamon
1 tsp (5 mL) dried tarragon
½ tsp (2.5 mL) dried thyme
1½ tsp (7.5 mL) saffron threads
2 medium potatoes, cooked and dry mashed

Melt butter in a pan and fry chopped onion until tender but not brown. Add all remaining ingredients and cook 3 minutes more. Remove from heat and use to stuff a 3 lb (1.5 kg) chicken.

A family favorite — roast chicken cooked with stuffing and a variety of vegetables.

Fillings

Most fillings can be prepared a couple of hours before serving. To reheat, arrange filled potatoes on a baking sheet and bake at 350°F (180°C) for 15 minutes (or microwave on HIGH 1 minute per potato).

MUSHROOM FILLING

6 Potato Cups (see recipe)
3 tbsp (45 mL) butter
¼ lb (110 g) mushrooms, sliced
grated strong Cheddar cheese

Prepare potato cups, reserving mashed potato pulp. Melt butter, add mushrooms and gently fry until tender (or microwave on HIGH 2 minutes). Combine mushrooms and potato and fill shells.

Top each shell with cheese. Heat until cheese topping is golden brown.

Fills 6 potatoes

CHICKEN AND ALMOND FILLING

6 Potato Cups (see recipe)
1½ tbsp (20 mL) butter
3 tbsp (45 mL) almond halves
½ lb (225 g) cooked chicken, diced
3 tbsp (45 mL) mayonnaise

Prepare potato cups, reserving mashed potato pulp. Melt butter, add almonds and fry until lightly browned. Combine with remaining ingredients. Spoon into shells and reheat.

Fills 6 potatoes

MEXICAN FILLING

6 Potato Cups (see recipe)
¼ cup (60 mL) canned baked beans
pinch chili powder
3 tbsp (45 mL) sour cream
grated Cheddar cheese
12 corn chips

Prepare potato cups, reserving mashed potato pulp. Combine baked beans, chili powder, sour cream and mashed potato. Spoon into shells and top with cheese. Reheat and brown cheese topping. Serve with two corn chips poked into the top of each filled potato.

Fills 6 potatoes

Potato Cups

SHRIMP FILLING

6 Potato Cups (see recipe)
3 tbsp (45 mL) butter, melted
½ lb (225 g) cooked shrimp, shelled,
   deveined and halved
1 tsp (5 mL) lemon juice
pepper to taste
1 tbsp (15 mL) chopped fresh chives

Prepare potato cups, reserving mashed potato pulp. Combine all ingredients. Spoon into shells and reheat.

Fills 6 potatoes

VEGETARIAN FILLING

6 Potato Cups (see recipe)
½ cup (125 mL) any green vegetables,
   cooked and chopped
1 tomato, chopped
1 tbsp (15 mL) mayonnaise

Prepare potato cups, reserving mashed potato pulp. Combine all ingredients. Spoon into shells and reheat.

Fills 6 potatoes

SOUR CREAM AND GREEN ONION FILLING

6 Potato Cups (see recipe)
1½ tbsp (20 mL) butter
2 green onions, diced
pepper to taste
½ cup (125 mL) sour cream

Prepare 6 potato cups, reserving mashed potato pulp. Melt butter and fry green onions until tender (or microwave on HIGH 2 minutes).

Add pepper, sour cream and mashed potato and mix well. Spoon mixture into the shells and reheat.

Fills 6 potatoes

BACON AND MUSHROOM FILLING

6 Potato Cups (see recipe)
4 slices bacon, diced
3 tbsp (45 mL) butter
¼ lb (110 g) mushrooms, sliced

Prepare potato cups, reserving mashed potato pulp. Fry bacon in butter until crisp (or microwave butter and bacon on HIGH 2-3 minutes). Combine bacon and mashed potato. Gently fry mushrooms until tender (or microwave on HIGH 2 minutes). Fold into potato mixture, spoon into shells and reheat.

Fills 6 potatoes

CHEESE AND MUSTARD FILLING

6 Potato Cups (see recipe)
3 tbsp (45 mL) diced ham
1 tbsp (15 mL) chopped fresh chives
2 tsp (10 mL) prepared mustard
¼ cup (60 mL) grated strong Cheddar cheese

Prepare potato cups, reserving mashed potato pulp. Combine all ingredients except cheese. Spoon into shells. Top with cheese. Reheat and brown cheese.

Fills 6 potatoes

TASTY VARIATION:
☐ Replace prepared mustard with 2 tsp (10 mL) Dijon mustard.

CELERIAC FILLING

6 Potato Cups (see recipe)
1½ tbsp (20 mL) butter
1 celeriac root, peeled and diced
pepper to taste
2 egg yolks, beaten
1 egg white, lightly whisked
6 slices Cheddar cheese

Prepare potato cups, reserving mashed potato pulp.

Melt butter, add celeriac and gently cook until tender (or microwave on HIGH 2 minutes). Combine celeriac, mashed potato, pepper, egg yolks and fold in egg white.

Spoon into shells. Top each potato shell with a slice of cheese, reheat and brown cheese.

Fills 6 potatoes

BLUE POTATO FILLING

6 Potato Cups (see recipe)
3 tbsp (45 mL) butter
1 cup (250 mL) mashed blue cheese
1 tbsp (15 mL) cream
1 tbsp (15 mL) tomato sauce or catsup
½ tsp (2.5 mL) chopped fresh basil

Prepare potato cups, reserving mashed potato pulp. Melt butter in a pan (or microwave on HIGH 30 seconds). Add remaining ingredients and beat well. Spoon into shells and reheat.

Fills 6 potatoes

SEAFOOD FILLING

6 Potato Cups (see recipe)
¼ lb (110 g) fish, cooked and flaked (see Note)
½ cup (125 mL) mayonnaise
3 tbsp (45 mL) chopped fresh parsley

Prepare potato cups, reserving mashed potato pulp. Combine all filling ingredients. Spoon into shells and reheat.

Fills 6 potatoes

Note: Any fish is suitable; smoked haddock or cod are particularly delicious.

CHEESE AND CHUTNEY FILLING

6 Potato Cups (see recipe)
3 tbsp (45 mL) butter
⅔ cup (165 mL) grated strong Cheddar cheese
1 tbsp (15 mL) chutney
1 celery stalk, finely diced

Prepare potato cups, reserving mashed potato pulp. Melt butter, add all filling ingredients and mix well. Spoon into shells and reheat.

Fills 6 potatoes

CURRIED EGG FILLING

6 Potato Cups (see recipe)
3 eggs, hard-boiled, peeled and chopped
¼ cup (60 mL) mayonnaise
1 tsp (5 mL) curry powder
1 tsp (5 mL) garam masala

Prepare potato cups, reserving mashed potato pulp. Combine all ingredients. Spoon into shells and reheat.

Fills 6 potatoes

CRUNCHY CHEESE AND APPLE FILLING

6 Potato Cups (see recipe)
⅔ cup (165 mL) mashed or crumbled blue cheese
1 green apple, cored and diced (leave peel on)
3 tbsp (45 mL) mayonnaise

Prepare potato cups, reserving mashed potato pulp. Combine all ingredients. Spoon into shells and reheat.

Fills 6 potatoes

SAVORY BEEF AND BEAN FILLING

The mashed potato from Potato Cups recipe is not used in this filling.

6 Potato Cups (see recipe)
1 tbsp (15 mL) oil
1 onion, diced
1 lb (450 g) ground beef
3 tbsp (45 mL) tomato sauce or catsup
3 tbsp (45 mL) Worcestershire sauce
2 stalks celery, diced
3 tbsp (45 mL) canned kidney beans, washed and drained (optional)
1 tbsp (15 mL) chopped fresh parsley

Prepare potato cups; set mashed potato pulp aside for use in another recipe.

Heat oil in a pan, add onion and fry until tender. Add beef, tomato sauce or catsup, Worcestershire sauce, celery and kidney beans and cook for 15 minutes (or microwave on HIGH, stirring occasionally, for 8 minutes or until cooked).

Drain off excess liquid. Add parsley. Spoon into shells and reheat.

Fills 6 potatoes

TOMATO AND SHRIMP FILLING

½ lb (225 g) cooked shrimp
juice of ½ lemon
1½ tbsp (20 mL) butter
1 tbsp (15 mL) oil
1 onion, diced
1 tbsp (15 mL) flour
4 tomatoes, chopped
1 tbsp (15 mL) tomato paste
1 cube chicken stock
½ cup (125 mL) water

Place shrimp in a bowl, squeeze lemon juice over shrimp and store in refrigerator until ready to use. If shrimp are large, slice in half lengthwise before marinating.

Melt butter and oil, add onion and fry until transparent. Stir in flour and cook 1 minute. (Alternatively, microwave butter, oil and onion on HIGH 2 minutes. Stir in flour and cook on HIGH 1 minute.)

Add tomatoes, tomato paste, stock cube and water and stir until sauce thickens. Simmer 5 minutes. (Alternatively, combine remaining ingredients, stir well and microwave on HIGH 5 minutes.)

Add shrimp and lemon juice and stir until heated through.

Serves 6

TASTY VARIATION:
☐ Replace shrimp and lemon juice with 4 slices bacon, diced and fried with onion.

Tasty Toppings

All our toppings are quick and easy to prepare. No one could accuse the potato of being boring when served with one or more of the following:

- sour cream
- cottage cheese
- fresh herbs
- melted cheese
- diced crispy bacon or ham
- finely diced chili peppers

- toasted sesame seeds
- finely diced fried onion
- fried onion and tomato
- fried mushrooms
- fried mushrooms and onion

1. Rub potato with oil and wrap in foil.

2. Cut a criss-cross pattern in the top of each potato.

3. Spoon sour cream over potatoes.

Baking Day

Potatoes appear in bread recipes in many countries around the world. Originally used in times of grain shortages, potato bread is both economical and nutritious. It also makes particularly good toast and croutons. Cakes, biscuits and yeast rolls also come up light and fluffy, and make a delicious change from more conventional recipes.

IRISH SODA BREAD

2 cups (250 g) flour
1 cup (250 mL) self-rising flour
1 tsp (5 mL) baking soda
pinch salt
½ tsp (2.5 mL) sugar
1½ tbsp (20 mL) butter
2 potatoes, cooked and mashed
1¼ cups (310 mL) warmed buttermilk
1 egg, beaten

Sift flours together in a bowl. Add baking soda, salt and sugar; mix well. Rub butter into flour until mixture resembles fine bread crumbs. Mix in mashed potato.

Make a well in the center and pour in combined buttermilk and beaten egg. Mix to a dough, form into a round loaf and place on a greased baking sheet. Using a knife, mark bread into eight pieces, dust the top with a little flour and bake at 350°F (180°C) for 30–40 minutes. Cool before serving. To make a soft crust, brush with melted butter while hot.

Makes 1 loaf

POTATO GALETTE

3 tbsp (45 mL) butter
1 onion, sliced
4 medium potatoes, cooked and mashed
1 egg, beaten
1 cup (250 mL) grated strong Cheddar cheese
½ tsp (2.5 mL) dry mustard

Melt butter, add onion and gently fry until transparent (or microwave on HIGH 2 minutes). Combine with mashed potato, egg, cheese and mustard. Spoon mixture into a greased cake pan. Bake at 350°F (180°C) for 45 minutes. Turn out and cut into wedges. Serve as an accompaniment to roasts.

Serves 6

POTATO YEAST BREAD

1 tbsp (15 mL) yeast
1½ tbsp (25 mL) sugar
¼ cup (60 mL) warm water
3 potatoes, cooked and mashed
1 cup (250 mL) plus 3 tbsp (45 mL) warm milk
3 tbsp (45 mL) butter
4 cups (1 L) flour
pinch salt
1 tbsp (15 mL) freshly chopped chives

In a small bowl, sprinkle yeast over 1 tsp (5 mL) sugar and the warm water. Stir and let stand until mixture is very frothy. In a large mixing bowl, combine yeast mixture, 3 tbsp (45 mL) warm milk and the mashed potatoes. Set aside in a draft-free, warm place for 20 minutes.

Boil remaining milk (or microwave on HIGH 2 minutes). Add butter and stir until melted. Allow to cool to lukewarm. Combine remaining tbsp (15 mL) sugar, the flour, salt, chives and mashed potato and add to the yeast mixture. Stir. Make a well in the center and add butter-milk mixture. Mix until combined. Turn dough out onto a floured board and knead well for 10 minutes until smooth and elastic.

Return dough to bowl, cover with a warm, damp cloth and let stand in a warm place until dough has doubled in size (1½–2 hours). Turn out onto a floured board and punch dough in center, knead a further 10 minutes and place in a greased loaf pan. Cover with a warm damp cloth and leave in a warm place 45 minutes to rise again.

Bake 15 minutes at 400°F (200°C), reduce heat to 350°F (180°C) and bake a further 45 minutes. Remove bread from pan when cool. This tastes best eaten the same day it is cooked.

Makes 1 loaf

Irish Soda Bread and Potato Yeast Bread

CARAWAY POTATO CAKES

1 cup (250 mL) flour
1½ tbsp (20 mL) butter
4 medium potatoes, cooked and dry
  mashed
¼ cup (60 mL) milk
1 tbsp (15 mL) caraway seeds

Place flour in a bowl and rub in butter until it resembles fine bread crumbs. Add mashed potatoes and milk and mix to a soft dough. Turn out onto a floured board and knead until smooth.

Roll dough in a circle approximately 1 inch (2.5 cm) thick. With a floured cookie cutter, cut dough into rounds. Brush with a little milk and sprinkle with caraway seeds. Bake at 350°F (180°C) for 30 minutes.

Serve with strips of cooked bacon or as an accompaniment to roasts. Alternatively, serve with Savory Sauce (see recipe).

Serves 6

TASTY VARIATION:
☐ Replace caraway seeds with 1 tbsp (15 mL) unsweetened coconut.

1. Place flour in bowl and rub in butter.

SAVORY SAUCE

1 tbsp (15 mL) oil
1 onion, sliced
½ lb (225 g) ground beef
2 tomatoes, chopped
1 clove garlic, crushed
1 tbsp (15 mL) chopped fresh parsley

Heat oil, add onion and fry until transparent. Add meat and stir until browned. Add tomatoes and garlic, simmering for 20 minutes (or microwave on HIGH 10 minutes, stirring once). Add parsley and serve.

Makes 1 cup (250 mL)

WARTIME VITAMIN C
During the Civil War, women packed potatoes in barrels filled with brine and sent them to the prisons and the front lines. By eating the potatoes with the skins on, soldiers were able to get the vitamin C they needed.

2. Turn mixture onto floured board and knead until smooth.

3. Cut dough into rounds with cookie cutter.

4. Brush with milk and sprinkle with caraway seeds.

5. Serve with strips of cooked bacon or savory sauce.

ORANGE DELIGHT

½ cup (125 mL) butter
½ cup (125 mL) sugar
grated rind of 1 orange
½ cup (125 mL) orange juice
2 eggs, lightly beaten
1½ cups (325 mL) self-rising flour
1 medium potato, peeled and grated

ICING
1 cup (250 mL) icing sugar
orange juice
1 tsp (5 mL) butter
lemon and orange rind, to decorate

Cream butter and sugar until light and creamy. Add orange rind, orange juice, eggs and flour. Squeeze potato dry and add to mixture. Stir well to combine. Spoon into a greased and lined 6½ inch (17 cm) round cake pan. Bake at 350°F (180°C) for 30 minutes. Test with skewer. It should come out clean when cake is cooked. Place a cake rack on top of pan. Turn pan upside-down so cake rests on rack. Remove pan and cool before icing.

To make icing, put icing sugar into a small pan and add sufficient orange juice to make a firm mixture. Beat in butter, heat on low very briefly (or microwave on HIGH 30 seconds) and spread over cake. Decorate with slivers of lemon and orange rind.

POTATO CRACKERS

¾ cup (180 mL) rolled oats
¾ cup (180 mL) flour
⅓ cup (85 mL) butter
2 medium potatoes, cooked and
   mashed

Combine oats and flour in a bowl. Rub in butter with fingertips, then knead in mashed potatoes to form a stiff dough.

Carefully roll out on a floured board, and cut out thin rounds using a cookie cutter or upside-down glass.

Cook on greased trays at 350°F (180°C) for 20 minutes or until crackers are crisp and lightly browned.

Makes 20

CHOCOLATE CAKE

¾ cup (180 mL) butter
½ cup (125 mL) sugar
½ tsp (2.5 mL) vanilla
2 eggs, beaten
½ tsp (2.5 mL) ground cinnamon
¼ tsp (1 mL) ground nutmeg
1½ cups (375 mL) self-rising flour
½ cup (125 mL) milk
1 medium potato, peeled and grated
3 oz (90 g) dark chocolate, grated
½ cup (125 mL) chopped hazelnuts

ICING 1
1 egg white, whisked
1 cup (250 mL) icing sugar
1 tsp (5 mL) cocoa
1 tsp (5 mL) water
grated dark chocolate, to sprinkle

ICING 2
½ cup (125 mL) butter
1½ cups (375 mL) icing sugar
1 tbsp (15 mL) cocoa
3 tbsp (45 mL) milk
grated dark chocolate, to sprinkle

To make cake, cream butter and sugar together until smooth. Add vanilla, eggs, spices, half the flour and half the milk. Stir well and mix in remaining flour and milk. Squeeze potato dry and stir into mixture with grated chocolate and hazelnuts.

Spoon mixture into a greased and lined loaf pan. Bake at 350°F (180°C) for 1 hour. Test with skewer to see if cake is done. It should come out clean when cake is cooked.

Place a cake rack on top of loaf pan, turn upside-down so cake rests on rack. Remove pan and cool cake thoroughly before icing.

If you choose to make Icing 1, combine stiffly beaten egg white, icing sugar, cocoa and water. Mix well and spread over cooled cake top. Garnish with grated chocolate.

If you choose to make Icing 2, cream butter until light and creamy. Add icing sugar, cocoa and milk. Beat well and spread over cake top. Garnish with grated chocolate.

POTATO ROLLS

1 medium potato, peeled and boiled
¼ cup (60 mL) sugar
½ cup (125 mL) butter
2 eggs, beaten
2 cups (500 mL) flour
1 tbsp (15 mL) yeast

Drain potato, reserving 1 cup (250 mL) of potato cooking water. Mash potato with sugar, butter, eggs and flour. Pour reserved cup of warm potato water in a bowl and stir in yeast. Let stand until dissolved and frothy. Make a well in the center of the mixture and pour in yeast and water. Mix well.

Turn out onto a floured board and knead for 10 minutes, adding extra flour if necessary to make a stiff dough. Place back in bowl, cover with a damp cloth and let stand in a draft-free, warm place until dough doubles in size.

Turn out again onto a floured board. Punch down and knead a further 10 minutes. Cut into 16 balls. Arrange balls on a greased tray, let stand in a warm place, covered, until balls double in size. Bake at 350°F (180°C) for 20-25 minutes. Serve as dinner or barbecue rolls.

Makes 16 rolls

VINCENT VAN GOGH
... surely must have been a potato-holic. Several of his masterpieces feature the potato, the most famous being 'The Potato Eaters,' painted in 1885. His paintings often show French peasants cultivating or peeling potatoes.

Orange Delight and Chocolate Cake

Sweet Potatoes

Although botanically quite distinct, sweet potatoes have been included in our book because they are extremely popular. Traditionally associated with Creole cooking, they can be used to make delicious sweet pies, fruit salads, baked dishes and accompaniments.

INDONESIAN FRUIT AND VEGETABLE SALAD

Use a variety of fruits and vegetables in season such as:
fresh pineapple
Granny Smith apples
oranges
grapefruit
mango
grapes
cucumber
sweet potato
radishes
celery
green onions

SALAD DRESSING
3 tbsp (45 mL) sugar
½ tsp (2.5 mL) salt
1 tbsp (15 mL) cider vinegar
1 tbsp (15 mL) vegetable oil

Peel fruits and vegetables and slice into bite-size pieces.

Arrange on large platter attractively or put into individual dishes.

Serve with dressing in a separate bowl. To make dressing, mix all ingredients together in a bowl.

COOKING SWEET POTATOES
To cook sweet potatoes, boil for 20 minutes or until tender. Or microwave on HIGH 6 minutes per 1 lb (450 g).
It's difficult to peel sweet potatoes before cooking them. Cook potatoes and then the skins can be easily removed.

SWEET POTATO PIE

PASTRY
2 cups (500 mL) flour
1 tbsp (15 mL) custard powder
1 tbsp (15 mL) icing sugar
¾ cup (180 mL) butter
1-3 tbsp (15–45 mL) water
1 tsp (5 mL) lemon juice

FILLING
1 lb (450 g) sweet potatoes, cooked, peeled and mashed
1 cup (250 mL) milk
2 eggs, beaten
½ cup (125 mL) brown sugar
1 tsp (5 mL) cinnamon
½ tsp (2.5 mL) nutmeg
1 tbsp (15 mL) melted butter

To make the pastry, sift flour, custard powder and icing sugar into a bowl. Using fingertips, mix in butter until mixture resembles fine bread crumbs. Using a knife, cut in water and lemon juice to make a firm dough and add more water if necessary.

Turn out on to a floured board, knead lightly and roll pastry out to fit an 8 inch (20 cm) pie plate. Carefully lift pastry into greased pie plate and refrigerate until required.

To make filling, combine all filling ingredients and beat until smooth. Spoon into pie shell. When pouring, hold a large spoon over the center and allow filling to spill over the spoon into the shell. This prevents pastry being weakened in the center.

Bake at 350°F (180°C) for ½ hour or until set. Serve with ice cream or whipped cream.

Serves 6

TASTY VARIATIONS:
☐ For filling, replace milk with 1¼ cups (310 mL) cream or sour cream;
☐ add 2 apples, peeled, cored, cooked and mashed, to potatoes.

Sweet Potato Pie

Sweet Potato Salad

SWEET POTATO SALAD

2 lbs (1 kg) sweet potatoes, peeled and diced
1 lb (450 g) potatoes, peeled and diced
1½ tbsp (20 mL) butter
2 onions, sliced
2 slices bacon, diced
2 hard-boiled eggs, shelled and sliced
½ cup (125 mL) French Dressing (see recipe)
½ cup (125 mL) sour cream

Combine both types of potato and boil for 20 minutes or until tender (or cover sweet potatoes with microwave-proof plastic wrap and cook on HIGH 3 minutes, then cover potatoes with microwave-proof plastic wrap and add 1 tsp (5 mL) water and cook on HIGH 5 minutes. Combine).

Melt butter, add onions and fry until tender. Add bacon and fry until crisp (or microwave butter, onion and bacon on HIGH 3 minutes).

Arrange potatoes, onions, bacon and eggs in a salad bowl. Combine French Dressing and sour cream, and pour over salad. Chill thoroughly. Serve with lettuce and tomatoes.

Serves 6

TASTY VARIATIONS:
☐ Add 1 green apple, cored and diced;
☐ add 2 tbsp (30 mL) chopped walnuts.

JAMAICAN CASSEROLE

This makes a delicious accompaniment to roasts and barbecued meats.

1 lb (450 g) sweet potatoes
3 tbsp (45 mL) butter
8 oz (220 g) canned crushed pineapple, drained
3 tbsp (45 mL) sherry or rum
½ tsp (2.5 mL) nutmeg
½ tsp (2.5 mL) cinnamon

Mash potatoes with butter. Stir in pineapple, sherry and spices. Spoon into a greased casserole and bake at 350°F (180°C) for 15 minutes (or microwave on MEDIUM 5 minutes).

Serves 6

SWEET POTATOES WITH APPLES

This dish goes well with roast or fried pork or ham.

¾ cup (180 mL) honey
⅓ cup (85 mL) butter
4 red apples, cored and sliced into rings
1¾ lb (800 g) sweet potatoes, cooked, peeled and dry mashed
juice of 2 oranges

In a frying pan heat together half the honey and half the butter (or microwave on HIGH 1 minute). Add sliced apples and cook for 3 minutes on each side (or microwave on HIGH 3 minutes).

Add orange juice, remaining butter and honey to potatoes, and mix well. Spoon potato on to six plates and top with cooked apples.

Serves 6

TASTY VARIATIONS:
☐ ¼ cup (60 mL) pecans
☐ 6 slices pineapple

BAKED SWEET POTATO

6 sweet potatoes, peeled and cut in half
oil

Arrange potatoes in an oiled baking dish and brush lightly with oil. Bake at 350°F (180°C) for 40 minutes (see *Note*).

Serves 6

Note: To bake quickly, parboil for 20 minutes (or microwave on HIGH, allowing 6 minutes per 1 lb (450 g). Let stand 1 minute). Finish in oven 20 minutes.

TASTY VARIATION:
☐ For roasted potatoes, arrange potatoes on a rack and bake without oil.

BUTTERED SWEET POTATOES

3 tbsp (45 mL) butter
1 tbsp (15 mL) flour
1 cup (250 mL) milk
1¾ lbs (800 g) sweet potatoes, cooked, peeled and diced
2 tsp (10 mL) cinnamon

Melt butter, stir in flour and cook for 1 minute. Remove from heat, stir in milk, return to heat, stir until mixture boils then remove. (Alternatively, microwave butter on HIGH 1 minute then add flour and cook on HIGH 1 minute. Stir in milk and cook on HIGH 2 minutes. Stir well.)

Arrange potatoes in a greased shallow casserole dish. Top with sauce. Sprinkle with cinnamon and serve immediately.

Serves 6

TASTY VARIATIONS:
☐ Replace cinnamon with 1 tsp (5 mL) ground cloves;
☐ before serving, sprinkle 3 tbsp (45 mL) grated cheese over top and brown under broiler (or microwave on HIGH until cheese bubbles).

SWEET POTATO LAYER

1 lb (450 g) sweet potatoes, peeled and sliced
2 onions, sliced
3 tomatoes, sliced
1 tbsp (15 mL) chopped fresh basil
2 cubes chicken stock
2 cups (500 mL) water
1 cup (250 mL) grated strong Cheddar cheese

Layer half the potatoes in the bottom of a greased casserole dish. Next, layer onions, tomatoes and basil and top with remaining potatoes. Crumble stock cubes and mix with the water. Pour over the casserole. Top with grated cheese. Bake at 350°F (180°C) for 1 hour (or microwave on HIGH 5 minutes, then MEDIUM 10 minutes). Serve warm as a complete meal.

Serves 6

TASTY VARIATIONS:
☐ To the tomato-onion layer add 1 carrot, peeled and sliced;
☐ add 1 lb (450 g) ground beef or lamb, cooked, to tomato-onion layer.

SWEET POTATO RING

2 lbs (1 kg) sweet potatoes, cooked and peeled
3 eggs, separated
3 tbsp (45 mL) melted butter
1 tsp (5 mL) ground ginger

TOPPING
4 slices stale bread, crusts removed, ground to make bread crumbs
3 tbsp (45 mL) brown sugar
2 tsp (10 mL) cinnamon
3 tbsp (45 mL) pecans

Mash potatoes with egg yolks, butter and ginger. Whisk egg whites until stiff and fold into mixture. Grease a ring pan and spoon in mixture (or place in a microwave-safe dish).

Combine topping ingredients. Sprinkle over potato mixture and bake at 350°F (180°C) for 20 minutes (or microwave on HIGH 5 minutes). Delicious with roasts or barbecues.

Serves 6

TASTY VARIATIONS:
☐ Add ⅓ cup (85 mL) mixed vegetables, cooked, to mashed potato and serve as a complete meal;
☐ replace butter with 1 tbsp (15 mL) orange juice and 1 tbsp (15 mL) pineapple juice.

CANDIED SWEET POTATOES

1 lb (450 g) sweet potatoes, cooked and peeled
¼ cup (60 mL) butter
1 cup (250 mL) brown sugar

Arrange potatoes in a greased baking dish. Melt butter and sugar together and pour over potatoes. Bake at 350°F (180°C) for 20 minutes, basting occasionally.

(Alternatively, melt butter and sugar together on HIGH 2 minutes. Pour mixture over potatoes, microwave on HIGH 3 minutes). Serve with roasts.

Serves 6

Buttered Sweet Potatoes

Children's Special Spuds

Appetizing though the potato undoubtedly is, all parents sometimes have trouble enticing their children to eat good food. The following recipes are designed especially to appeal to children, visually and tastewise.

EGGS IN CARS

2 large potatoes, peeled
4 hard-boiled eggs, shelled
8 raisins
16 cherry tomatoes
2 slices cucumber
1 carrot, grated
1 cup (250 mL) peas, cooked
1 cup (250 mL) grated cheese

Boil potatoes for 20 minutes or until tender (or microwave on HIGH for 6–8 minutes). Cut each potato in half lengthwise. Place potato half cut-side down on a plate. Scoop out a hole large enough to support egg, approximately ¾ inch (2 cm) deep. Using a sharp knife, pierce 2 small holes in egg for eyes, insert raisins. Set egg in potato.

Arrange two tomatoes as wheels on each side of potato half. Cut cucumber slices in half. Using a sharp knife make a small slit in potato in front of egg and insert half cucumber slice, cut side down. Arrange grated carrot, as hair, on top of egg. Arrange 2 rows of peas as road, in front and behind car, placing grated cheese in between rows of peas. Repeat with remaining ingredients.

Makes 4

SPUD'S FUNNY FACE

1 large potato, baked or boiled with skin on
1 raw carrot, peeled and washed
1 tbsp (15 mL) cooked peas

Cut a small slice from both ends of the potato. Cut off about ½ inch (1 cm) of the carrot's pointed end. Grate remaining carrot. Sit the potato on its end on a plate.

Carefully make two small holes for eyes and place a pea in each. Make a hole for the nose and push in the flat carrot end. Make a slit for the mouth and fill with a strip of grated carrot. Pile grated carrot on top for hair. Surround potato with peas and carrot. Heat in the oven at 350°F (180°C) for 10 minutes (or microwave on HIGH 1–2 minutes).

Serves 1

FUNNY/SAD POTATO FACE

4 potatoes, peeled
1 tbsp (15 mL) butter
3 tbsp (45 mL) milk
1 egg
8 slices cucumber
4 cherry tomatoes
2 hard-boiled eggs, sliced
4 cocktail wieners, cooked
8 lettuce leaves
alfalfa, to garnish
green onion, sliced, to garnish

Chop potatoes and boil in water for 20 minutes or until tender (or microwave in a freezer bag on HIGH for 10–12 minutes). Add butter, milk and egg and mash until smooth.

To make funny face spread ¼ of potato mixture on a dinner plate. Use 2 cucumber slices for eyes and sliced green onion for the nose. Cut a cherry tomato in half and place with cut sides down as cheeks. Use egg slices as ears. Cut a wiener in half lengthwise and place with curve upwards for a smiling mouth or curve downwards for a sad mouth. Make hair with two lettuce leaves and alfalfa sprouts. Repeat with remaining ingredients.

Makes 4

Eggs in Cars, Spud's Funny Face, Oven Baked Fries, and Funny/Sad Potato Face

OVEN-BAKED FRIES

2 medium potatoes, peeled and washed
3 tbsp (45 mL) oil

Cut potatoes into strips and pat dry with paper towels. Arrange strips on oiled baking sheet. Sprinkle with oil and bake at 475°F (250°C) for 30 minutes, turning once.

Serves 2

Bubble and Squeak

Last but by no means least, there are leftovers. So potentially useful, so irritatingly wasteful when you have to throw them away.

LEFTOVER SOUP

11 oz (310 g) canned red kidney beans, drained
1 medium potato, peeled and diced
1 onion, diced
1 carrot, peeled and diced
1 zucchini, diced
1 stalk celery, diced
2 cups (500 mL) canned tomatoes, liquid reserved
1 cube chicken stock
water

Rinse kidney beans in cold water. Place in a pan with all vegetables, stock cube and sufficient water to cover. Bring to a boil, lower heat and simmer 1 hour. Serve in individual bowls with toast.

Serves 6

HOMEMADE SAUSAGES

½ lb (225 g) cooked meat or chicken, finely ground or diced
1½ tbsp (20 mL) butter, melted
2 green onions, finely chopped
1 tbsp (15 mL) chopped fresh parsley
3 tbsp (45 mL) water
1 cube beef or chicken stock
1 tsp (5 mL) flour
2 eggs, beaten
4 medium potatoes, cooked and mashed with 3 tbsp (45 mL) butter
oil for frying

Combine meat, butter, green onions, parsley, water and stock cube in a pan. Bring to a boil, then lower heat and simmer until water evaporates. Remove from heat and stir in flour and eggs. Mix well, return to heat and stir until thickened. Mix in mashed potatoes.

Spoon mixture into a greased casserole dish and refrigerate overnight. Next day, turn out onto a floured board and roll spoonfuls of mixture into tiny sausage shapes.

Heat oil and fry sausages on both sides until crisp and brown. Serve as appetizers with a barbecue.

Serves 6

BUBBLE AND SQUEAK

A traditional favorite in Britain and other countries around the world – the unusual name comes from the noise it makes in the pan while cooking!

2 slices bacon
1 onion, sliced
1 medium potato, cooked and mashed
¼ cabbage, shredded and lightly steamed

Cook bacon slices then remove with a slotted spoon. Add onions to pan and gently fry until tender. Add potato and cabbage. Press together to form a large cake. Cook until first side is brown. Turn with a spatula and brown on other side. Serve on toast or with eggs.

Serves 6

PATTA CAKE

The name refers to patting the mixture between the palms of the hands to form a flat cake.

4 medium potatoes, cooked and mashed
3 tbsp (45 mL) milk
1 tbsp (15 mL) self-rising flour
½ lb (225 g) cooked ground meat
oil for frying

Mash potatoes with milk. Add flour and mix to a stiff dough, adding more milk if necessary. Divide mix into six portions.

Press one portion out with your hand to make a circle. Fill with a spoonful of meat, fold and press edges closed. Gently press in palms till flattened. Repeat with remaining meat and potato mixtures.

Heat oil and fry cakes until lightly browned on both sides. Serve with bacon or green salad.

Serves 6

Patta Cake and Leftover Soup

How to Grow Your Own

Potatoes

The potato or Irish potato (*Solanum tuberosum*) originated in the temperate regions of the Andes in South America where it has been used by the native people as food for some 2000 years.

The potato plant is a perennial herb with straggling, semi-erect branches bearing leaves with three or four pairs of oval-shaped leaflets. The flower is white or purplish and develops into a small, green tomato-like berry. The plant has fibrous roots and many rhizomes or underground stems which become swollen at the tip to form the edible tubers. The tubers are also used for planting and are commonly referred to as 'seed potatoes.'

Potatoes are a very adaptable crop but prefer temperate or cool climates. However, the plants are extremely susceptible to frost. In warm regions, potatoes can be planted at almost any time of the year, but early autumn, winter or early spring planting is recommended. In temperate climates an early crop can be planted in spring and a late crop planted in mid-summer. In cold climates, plantings are made in late spring or mid-summer only, so that the plants are fully grown before cold weather arrives.

Potatoes are adaptable to both light and heavy soils but good drainage is essential. Prepare the bed to spade depth well before planting so that the soil is in friable condition for the tubers to expand evenly.

Tubers for planting should be 1–2 ozs (30-60 g) in weight. Large tubers can be cut into block-like pieces provided there is at least one 'eye', or sprout, on each piece. Always buy seed potatoes harvested from crops free of virus and other diseases. Good seed potatoes are available from plant nurseries and garden stores in late winter or early spring. Where two crops can be grown in one year save some tubers from the most productive plants in

Digging potatoes

the early crop for later planting.

Before planting, spread the tubers or cut pieces in a shady spot for a week or two. This greening hardens the sprouts and makes them less liable to damage. Discard any tubers which develop spindly shoots or other blemishes. About 5 or 6 lbs (2-3 kg) of seed potatoes is enough for 40 to 60 plants. If the crop is well grown, this should provide enough potatoes for the average family for an entire year.

Make the planting furrows about 6 inches (15 cm) deep and space them 24-30 inches (60-75 cm) apart. Sprinkle fertilizer along the bottom and cover with 2 inches (5 cm) of soil from the sides. Set the tubers or pieces of tubers on the soil layer in the furrow about 12 inches (30 cm) apart, then fill in with the remaining soil and rake the bed level. Potato plants will break the surface in about three weeks.

Cultivate between the rows to destroy weeds and gradually hill soil against the plants as they grow. This supports the sprawling stems and prevents greening of tubers formed close to the surface. Additional fertilizer is seldom necessary but the plants must be watered regularly to promote smooth, well-developed tubers.

Potatoes are ready for digging in 16 to 20 weeks from planting. For 'new' potatoes, you can start digging when the lower leaves turn yellow – usually about three weeks after the plants have flowered. Potatoes for storage should not be lifted until the plants have died off completely. After removing the soil from the potatoes, discard any showing skin damage or blemishes. Store your potatoes in a cool, airy place which must also be dark to prevent greening. Wooden boxes and cardboard cartons from which light is excluded or thick burlap bags are good containers for storage.

Diseases and pests
Early blight (target spot) and late blight (Irish blight) cause leaf spotting and can seriously damage plants and reduce yields. Always use seed potatoes from disease-free plants. Many virus diseases are transmitted by aphids, and regular sprays of recommended chemicals will control these insects and help to

prevent virus transmission. Infected plants should be removed and burned.

The Colorado Potato beetle is the worst insect pest of potatoes in the United States and Canada. The small larvae of the beetle will attack the potato foliage. Search for and destroy the egg clusters in early spring. (They are bright orange.) Later, the black and orange beetles will appear. These can be picked off the plants and destroyed.

Sweet Potatoes

The sweet potato (*Ipomoea batatas*) is thought to have originated in South America but was also recorded by early explorers in the East Indies and the Philippine Islands. The plants are perennials with trailing vines bearing a dense mass of arrow-shaped leaves. The edible, under-ground tubers may be creamy-white, buff, brown, pink or purple in color. The flesh is usually yellow but some cultivars have white or pink flesh. The sweet potato is a major crop in countries with warm, temperate, subtropical or tropical climates, and the cooked tubers are especially valued as high-energy foods because of their starch and sugar content.

Sweet potatoes are often confused with yams. The yam (Dioscorea batatas) is also a perennial vine with edible tubers which may reach 24-40 inches (60-100 cm) in length. The cultivation of yams is confined to some tropical countries and the islands of the Pacific Ocean.

As the sweet potato is a warm season plant, it is susceptible to frost, and requires a growing season of about six months. Its cultivation is not recommended in cool temperate or cold regions. In the home garden, the rambling vines need a lot of space to grow.

Light soils or those enriched with organic matter to provide a friable structure are most suitable. The soil is prepared in much the same way as for potatoes. Sweet potato plants are started from shoots or cuttings from tubers. Unlike potatoes, which are stem tubers with a number of eyes, sweet potatoes are root tubers which produce new shoots at the top of the tuber in the same way as dahlias. Shoots or cuttings may be

available in late winter or early spring from plant nurseries. Or tubers can be purchased and buried in a box of moist sand. Keep the box in a warm spot, and shoots will soon develop. When the shoots are 4–6 inches (10-15 cm) long, carefully separate them from the parent tuber for transplanting.

After spreading fertilizer along the line where the plants are to grow, rake it into the topsoil and form a ridge about 4 inches (10 cm) above the garden bed for planting the shoots. Space the shoots about 12 inches (30 cm) apart and allow 24–30 inches (60-75 cm) between rows. For the average family 20 to 24 plants should be sufficient.

Cultivate between plants and rows to control weeds until the vines cover the soil in between. Water the vines regularly and lift them up occasionally to prevent roots developing at the nodes (joints) of the vines. New plants formed at the nodes tend to restrict tuber development under the parent plant. Additional fertilizer is rarely necessary.

Tubers should not be dug until the plants are yellow and die back. Tuber quality improves with maturity, but if cold weather or frost is expected, dig the tubers immediately. Tubers subjected to low temperatures (50°F [10°C] or less) will be damaged and will not store well. After digging, leave the vines and tubers in heaps to cure for about a week, covering the heaps with burlap or plastic bags at night to avoid low temperature damage. Mature tubers have a firm skin and, when cut with a knife, the surface dries quickly and cleanly. If the tubers are not mature, a milky sap exudes from the cut surface which discolors to a dark green on drying. Before storing, discard any tubers with blemishes or symptoms of rotting. Store sweet potatoes in a warm, dry place; the storage temperature must not fall below 50°F (10°C).

Diseases and pests
Sweet potatoes are remarkably free of diseases and pests. Control leaf-eating caterpillars with recommended chemicals. The mass of dense foliage must be sprayed thoroughly.

Glossary

INGREDIENTS

BREAD CRUMBS

Soft: fresh bread crumbs, made with one- or two-day-old bread in a blender or food processor.

Dry: commercial packaged bread crumbs.

BULGUR: a precooked cracked wheat, available at supermarkets, delicatessens and health food stores. It is also known as bulkar (Arabic), pourgouri (Greek) and bular (Turkish).

BUTTER: use salted butter unless otherwise specified.

CABBAGE: use green cabbage unless otherwise specified, for example red cabbage or white cabbage.

PEPPERS: sweet peppers, red and green.

CHEESES

Cheddar: most of the recipes call for strong cheddar (also called 'old' or 'aged'). It performs better in cooked dishes than unaged cheddar.

Munster: substitute Brie if Munster is unavailable.

CHICKPEA FLOUR: a flour made with ground chickpeas, available at health food and ethnic stores.

CHILI: use fresh chili peppers where specified, but treat them with great care. Rubber gloves can protect the skin from burning. Make sure you never touch your eyes while preparing chili peppers. The seeds are the hottest part; they can be removed and discarded, if you prefer. Chili peppers come in all degrees of hot; you might want to ask the produce manager which peppers are the hottest and which the most mild.

CREAM: there are different kinds of cream, and the difference depends on the butterfat content of the cream. Whipping cream is between 32 and 40 percent butterfat; medium cream or coffee cream is 18 percent; half and half cream is 12 percent. Unless a recipe specifies which kind to use, choose between coffee cream and half and half.

Sour cream: dairy sour cream. Also available in a fat-reduced form which has fewer calories.

FLOUR: use all-purpose flour unless otherwise stated. Some recipes call for rice flour, which is available in health food stores. Whole wheat flour is also available in health food stores, and in some grocery stores. Self-rising flour is all-purpose flour to which baking powder has been added in the proportions of 1 cup (125 g) flour to 2 tsp (10 mL) baking powder. It is available in the baking aisle in most grocery stores. Potato flour and chick pea flour can be found in health food stores.

FRUIT: we specify fresh or canned, but if no fresh fruit is available, you can substitute canned or frozen. The dish may taste slightly different.

GARAM MASALA: an Indian blend of spices, available in ethnic and health food stores. Its main ingredients are ground coriander, cumin, and chili peppers.

GHEE: a type of clarified butter made by heating ordinary unsalted butter to remove the impurities. Ghee is the yellow liquid which remains when the foam and sediment are removed.

GINGER ROOT: fresh ginger root is available in the produce department of most grocery stores. Usually it is peeled and crushed before it is added to a recipe. To make its preparation easier, you can crush it in a garlic press. Or chop finely, then add. If you can't find fresh ginger root, you can substitute powdered ginger. Use 1 teaspoon (5 mL) of dried for every tablespoon (15 mL) of fresh called for in the recipe.

GREEN ONIONS: very small onions with small white bulbs and long green stems. The stems are also used. They are sometimes called spring onions, scallions or shallots.

HERBS: our recipes specify whether to use fresh or dried herbs. If you need to replace fresh herbs with dried, the ratio is 1 tsp (5 mL) of dried to 1 tbsp (15 mL) fresh herbs.

MIXED SPICE: a finely ground spice combination that includes allspice, nutmeg and cinnamon; used to flavor cakes and buns.

MUSHROOMS, DRIED: available from supermarkets and delicatessens, they need to be soaked for 20 minutes before using.

OIL: use a vegetable or olive oil, unless otherwise specified.

PAPPADUMS: thin crisp Indian wafer bread made from spiced potato or rice flour. They are best cooked by frying in oil but can also be baked.

PROSCIUTTO HAM: a fine quality cured ham from Italy. The ham is rubbed with salt, sugar, nitrates, pepper, allspice, nutmeg, coriander and mustard. It is packed for 10 days, and then the process is repeated. Upon maturing, the ham is pressed, steamed and rubbed with pepper. Local tradition maintains that the hams get their flavor by prolonged aging in the mountain air.

PUMPKIN: the pumpkins to use in our recipes are sugar pumpkins. They are vastly smaller than their jack-o'lantern cousins (although sugar pumpkins make great jack-o'lanterns, too).

RICE FLOUR: available in the baking section of most supermarkets. It is used as a thickening agent.

SAUCES

Hoisin sauce: Chinese sauce made from onions, garlic and salted black beans.

Soy sauce: made from soya beans; many varieties of soy sauce are available, especially from Asian food stores. Experiment to find which one you prefer to use with different foods.

SEMOLINA: the hard part of the wheat sifted out of flour. Available in most supermarkets in the flour section.

STOCK CUBE: bouillon cube; can be replaced with 1 tsp (5 mL) powdered stock or bouillon.

SUGAR

Use any sugar you prefer unless the recipe specifies a specific type. The most common types are the following:

Granulated: fine white granulated sugar.
Raw: brown granulated sugar.
Brown: soft, moist sugar.
Icing: confectioner's or powdered sugar.

TAHINI: a paste made from crushed sesame seeds. It can be bought from delicatessens and some health food shops.

TARAMA: salted fish roe. Available from supermarkets and delicatessens.

YEAST: in our recipes, we use dry active yeast. In general, use 1 tbsp (15 mL) yeast for every 4 cups (1 L) of flour called for. Yeast can also be purchased in compressed cakes, which contain ⅔ oz (20 g). To use a cake of yeast, crumble into the warm water and stir with a fork, then let proof. Use one cake of yeast to replace 2 tsp (10 mL) dry active.

YOGURT: use plain yogurt.

Oven Temperatures

	Fahrenheit	Celsius
Very slow	250	120
Slow	275-300	140-150
Moderately slow	325	160
Moderate	350	180
Moderately hot	375	190
Hot	400	200
	425	220
	450	230
Very hot	475-500	250-260

Measurements

Standard Metric Measures

1 cup	=	250 mL
1 tbsp	=	15 mL
1 tsp	=	5 mL

All spoon measurements are level

Cup Measures

1 cup =	Ounces	Grams
bread crumbs, dry	4½	125
soft	2	60
butter	8¾	250
cheese, grated		
cheddar	4½	125
coconut, unsweetened	3¼	95
flour, cornstarch	4¾	130
plain or self-rising	4½	125
whole wheat	4¾	135
fruit, mixed dried	5¾	160
honey	12¾	360
sugar, granulated	8¾	250
icing	6¾	175
moist brown	6	170
nuts	4	125

Freshly dug potatoes

Potatoes make a good commercial crop

Coo-ee Picture Library

Index